RIGHTEOUS RECRUITING

ESSAYS ON REINVENTING TALENT ACQUISITION FOR PEOPLE

LIZ RYAN

TABLE OF CONTENTS

Part One: The Mindset

Part Two: The Process

Part Three: The Interview

PART ONE

THE MINDSET

INTRODUCTION

I love recruiting.

Recruiting thousands of incredible people is among the best things I've had the chance to do in my career.

It's fun to meet new people.

It's fun to sell your organization to people who have choices about where to work and who to work with.

I got to see what happens to an organization when you hire amazing people and set them loose to accomplish things far more ambitious than whatever you planned for.

Working as an HR leader for ten thousand years I learned that if your organization has a great energy and culture, recruiting becomes much easier.

Then you don't miss your product launch dates or sales targets. When your culture is healthy, people bring their friends to work alongside them.

Every part of running the business gets easier.

The word about your company travels. People want to work there.

When recruiting is difficult, it means there is a blockage in the forward energy of your organization – like a logjam in what should be a rushing river.

It is our job as leaders to figure out what's not working and fix it. Sometimes that involves telling the emperor or some lesser noble they are not wearing clothes. The more often you do that, the easier it gets.

Because selling leaders on the need to modernize and humanize recruiting is such an important part of our roles as HR people and recruiters, in this book I talk about how to speak up when everybody else in the room is silent - and how to tell your internal and external recruiting clients when they're drifting away from the real world.

You cannot be a good recruiter or HR person without taking a deep breath and speaking your truth to someone who sits higher on the organizational chart than you do (and doesn't want to hear what you have to say) on a regular basis.

I hope this book inspires you to say something that needs to be said!

The good news is that when you speak up for a righteous cause (like making your organization and its recruiting systems more nimble, smart and responsive) you get stronger, too.

Your muscles get huge.

That's what I want for you – huge muscles! I wrote this book to inspire you to step into your power as a leader who knows the impact of a human-centric recruiting process, and advocates for it.

I was lucky. As a young HR person my CEO told me, "Go out and find amazing people and hire them. Our team and culture are the only competitive advantages we've got."

I originally wrote these stories for publications or the Human Workplace blog.

I have updated and changed them for this RIGHTEOUS RECRUITING collection.

I hope these stories shift your thinking about recruiting or, if you were already on board with the Human Workplace worldview of recruiting as a human activity, I hope this book reinforces that knowledge and helps you sell the idea of human-based recruiting to anybody in your firm who needs to get the message.

Here's to you and your Righteous Recruiting adventures!

Liz Ryan
Boulder, Colorado

WANT TO HIRE GREAT PEOPLE? DO THESE TEN THINGS WELL

Recruiting is all about supply and demand.

It should not be as hard as it is – hard on recruiters and HR people, hard on candidates and hard on department managers.

It is hard to tell the truth about the things that make recruiting so challenging, because they are soft and sticky things like realistic vs. unrealistic hiring expectations, managerial quirks and slow, cumbersome recruiting pipelines.

Recruiting gets easier with every bit of truth we tell.

HR people can begin the truth-telling by being honest with hiring managers when they say, "I want someone with 15 years of experience and a master's degree, and I want to pay them $45,000 a year."

That's the moment when an HR person has to say, "That is a fantasy, my friend! Double the salary or cut the requirements in half, and we'll be in business!"

HR people have to speak up, and then recruiting will become much easier.

If time is money, then why aren't managers held accountable for the months that go by while job vacancies remain unfilled? Would you let managers slide so easily if they let your warehouses sit empty for months?

Value-creating employees are more valuable than raw materials or finished product sitting in a warehouse, so why don't we freak out and demand accountability when jobs go unfilled for so long?

Why do we see it is as a good thing when a manager is so "choosy" in their hiring process that dozens of candidates are considered (and their time wasted) and not one of them is found acceptable?

That's a failing on the manager's part, and on the part of the HR person who enabled the manager in their delusion.

I used to tell managers, "Get rid of half these Essential Requirements, and I will post this job ad for you." Either they could choose which half of the unnecessary bullets to whack, or else I would do it.

Recruiting must be easy because if it is hard, then there is something wrong with your recruiting process.

Jobs must be designed to be reasonable and they must pay what the market dictates.

If you need a plumber and you're willing to pay the market rate, you can find a plumber in an hour or two.

If you aren't willing to pay the market rate or if your requirements are unreasonable -- for instance, if you expect the plumber to train your puppy to roll over and fetch while he's fixing your sink -- you won't be able to find anyone to take the job.

That's your signal from Mother Nature -- you are out of touch!

Here are 10 great things you can do for your company, employees, customers, shareholders and yourself. If you do these 10 things well, you won't have to worry about recruiting.

Talented people will seek out your company because the word will have spread that you've created a great place to work.

Your employees will tell their friends to come and work for you. If your employee referrals are not delivering at least 20% of your new hires each year, something is wrong.

Your culture is off or you're making it too hard for your employees to recommend their friends for employment with confidence. That's an easy logjam to push out of the way!

Ten Ways to Make Recruiting Easy

1. Get rid of pointless bureaucratic policies that make your employees feel like prisoners instead of value-creators. The more your employees like their jobs, the easier your recruiting task will be.

2. Pay people fairly, at the middle or above the middle of the market range.

3. Give your employees latitude in the way they perform their jobs. Get rid of fussy step-by-step procedures unless they are required for safety or regulatory reasons. Your employees are smarter than your policy manual is, and more sensitive to nuance!

4. Train and reinforce your managers in leading through trust rather than fear. Take away whatever power your managers may have to write people up and put them on performance improvement plans. Teach them to coach and problem-solve with employees instead of using discipline to browbeat people into getting better at their jobs.

5. Make your work environment fun and breezy by backing off on hard-and-fast arrival and departure times and by paying people for their work, not for the hours they sit in their chair.

6. Make your organization a Swiss Cheese company by creating channels and pathways for communication up, down and sideways. Install a confidential telephone hotline your teammates can use to report bad things that happen at work and give every employee access to senior management so that problems can be acted on quickly without fear of recrimination.

7. Empower your HR people to become Ministers of Culture and to focus on making your company a

tremendous place to work rather than focusing on enacting and enforcing rules and policies.

8. Soften and humanize your recruiting process by getting rid of unnecessary steps and delays and making it fun and easy for people to learn about and pursue jobs in your company.

9. Shift out of scripted, formal interviews into conversational interviews that give both your interviewers and your candidates a chance to talk freely and honestly about the role and the intersection with the candidate's background and goals.

10. Talk about culture all the time, at every meeting and in every managerial communication -- and when you talk about it, be honest!

Make the topics of fear and trust everyday topics of conversation, because we deal with them both every day!

Make your company a little less mechanical and a little more human every day and watch how your employees respond. You won't worry about recruiting then -- or retention, or turnover, or poor morale or low productivity, either. It isn't rocket science, but it takes some work.

There is no time to waste!

WHERE ARE ALL THE GOOD JOB CANDIDATES HIDING?

Dear Liz,

I could use some advice on my company's recruiting program.

I run the entire HR function so recruiting is only one of my tasks, but at any given time I have six to fourteen job openings to fill so we are always on the hunt for good people.

I've used social media, traditional job boards, word-of-mouth and contingency recruiters to find candidates and I am coming up short.

One of my job openings has been open for almost seven months.

That particular department manager is very choosy, so that's part of the problem, but in general I find it difficult to get good candidates.

We end up sending out a lot of "no thanks" letters because quite a few of the people we interview are not as sharp or savvy as we need our new hires to be.

What do you recommend?

Is there an excellent careers site we should be using?

Thanks,
Natascha

Dear Natascha,

The hardest and most important part of solving any big, thorny problem is also the first step.

The first step in solving a big, thorny problem is to see our own part in creating it.

Let's think about the talent market.

The talent market is the imaginary (but very real) place where employers and job seekers find one another and decide to work together.

The talent market is a marketplace like any other -- like the stock market or a farmer's market where they sell fresh fruits and vegetables.

If a farmer showed up at the farmer's market with a truckload of overripe fruit and couldn't sell it, the farmer would know that shoppers were not to blame.

The farmer would know that their wares were sub-par that week, and they'd get their fruit to market faster the next time.

For some reason it is difficult for we employers to see that when we run job ads and nobody responds -- nobody we would consider hiring, in any case -- it's not the job applicants who are to blame?

Job ads are advertisements, no different from ads in the newspaper or your phone.

You are trying to get the attention of busy job seekers who have many employers to choose from.

Something in your offering is off kilter.

You say in your letter that the candidates you choose to interview are too often less than "sharp and savvy."

It is very easy to cast aspersions, but how can we accuse other people of being insufficiently savvy when your team hasn't mastered the simple task of staffing your organization -- especially given the number of talented job-seekers on the market?

There is no magical recruiting website that will bring you the imaginary candidates you seek.

I have a feeling that your third-party recruiters have been trying to tell you what I am telling you now: it is your side of the talent equation that is broken -- the demand side.

Here is a list of ten places to begin your investigation into how your recruiting process is broken.

Any or all of these culprits may be keeping you from filling your job openings quickly:

Ten Reasons Companies Have Trouble Filling Job Openings

1. Your job specs may be unrealistic.

2. Your salary and/or employee benefit programs may be too skimpy to attract great candidates.

3. Your working environment -- both the physical plant and the warmth and energy in your workplace, or lack thereof -- may be working against you.

4. Your job ads may be written in a terse, unfriendly way that emphasizes the many Essential Requirements job candidates need to bring you, without a word about why anyone would want the job.

5. Your application process may be driving the most talented folks (the ones with the healthiest self-esteem level) away.

6. Your screening interviews may be screening out talented people for silly reasons (e.g., they don't have the exact type of degree your department manager specified, or they lack experience with a software tool that they could learn in half a day).

7. Your standards for "sharp and savvy people" may be skewed. Are you working closely with your department managers to make sure they aren't turning the hiring process into an exercise in ego gratification, as too many hiring authorities do?

8. Your company may have a reputation as a bad place to work. Read your company reviews on Glass Door to find out.

9. You may be missing out on what should be your fastest and most fertile recruiting channel -- your own employees, customers and vendors.

    If your company is a great place to work, your employees will be happy to refer their friends to work for you, too.

    If that's not happening, your culture is very likely the problem.

10. You may be treating job candidates badly in the recruiting pipeline. Great people will not stick around to be abused. Another employer will value them (and their time and energy) more than you do!

Do not feel that I am bashing your program, because I don't know a thing about your recruiting process or your culture and beyond that, I am on your side.

However, I know that if you pay people correctly, treat them well during the hiring process and build a human culture where employees are valued, you will never have trouble filling job openings.

Recruiting is ruled by the laws of supply and demand.

The companies that have trouble recruiting are confused in some way about what the supply side of the talent market requires.

Your colleague who has taken seven months to hire a new employee because he's being "choosy" is doing your company, your customers and all of your stakeholders a grave disservice.

If his job opening were not essential to your company's success seven months ago, it should never have been approved.

Why is it acceptable in your culture for that manager to be seven months behind on the mission-critical project of filling that job?

Would it be okay for him to be seven months behind on any other business project? Why have you allowed recruiting to become your fellow managers' lowest priority?

This is a great time for you to step up in altitude and own your recruiting practice from stem to stern.

Take it up a big notch and remember that your employer brand and your customer-facing brand are the same thing.

There is only one community out there -- not two separate communities of job seekers on the one hand and customers on the other.

It's time to take a step back, own your recruiting problem and step into the adventure of reinventing your recruiting process to bring in the brilliant value creators you seek. We are cheering you on!

Best,
Liz

HOW TECHNOLOGY KILLED RECRUITING

I am more than old enough to remember the frenzy to automate every business process in the 1980s and nineties.

I remember the mantra, repeated many times a day: "Garbage in, garbage out."

Before you automated a process, every business analyst and programmer told us, it had to be a sensible process on its own.

If we had followed that wisdom, we wouldn't have the mess that we have in recruiting today.

We took a 1940s process, the job-application-screening process used by factories probably since Henry Ford was building Model Ts, and simply threw it online.

It was a garbage process, totally unsuited to the age of Knowledge Work, and we didn't change it A BIT before installing it in every Applicant Tracking System ever built.

And then, we fell asleep – so the process has never been updated since!

If any one of the vendors who built the first Applicant Tracking Systems had spent ten seconds thinking about that process, they would have designed it intelligently, using normal human logic to create a funnel that would simplify the process of separating the best candidates from the rest of the candidates in the selection pipeline.

That's not what they did, though.

When you fill out an online job application, it asks you where you worked and for how long, and it asks for your job title. Any reasonable person can extrapolate your major duties from the job title, but every ATS I've ever seen asks for the **tasks and duties** you performed, anyway.

Tasks and duties! As a candidate applying for a job you are asked what tasks and duties you performed, as though the list of items in a job description is more important for your next employer to understand than what you actually accomplished on the job.

A friend of mine is an elementary-school principal. She got halfway through completing an online job application in a recent job search and gave up. "It's so stupid, I couldn't even finish it," she said. "When the form asked me for my last position, I typed in 'Principal.' When the next field to complete was 'Tasks and duties,' I wanted to type in 'Don't YOU GUYS know?'"

If you think about the smartest, most switched-on person you've ever worked with, and then think about the biggest slacker and do-nothing person you've ever worked alongside, the contrast between those two people is obvious.

Yet no ATS in the world could distinguish between them, as long as the two people worked at the same job in the same company at the same time.

Applicant tracking systems don't inquire about what you learned at a job, what you left in your wake or what you view as your greatest accomplishment. Our selection mechanism is stuck in the Machine Age, interested only in the tasks and duties and tools you used, as though those things out of context could have any significance to your next boss at all.

It's not just the choice of fields in Applicant Tracking Systems that makes them useless and talent-repelling. They are built on bad logic at their core.

They are based on the notion that the central problem in recruiting is to screen out and dismiss unsuitable candidates, making a business function (and an expensive one at that!) out of the vetting process, whereas in fact the problem in recruiting is that it's hard to find great people, and we should be selling them throughout the process if we want them to consider joining us.

(And they are based on the idea that the best way to screen candidates in or out is by using keywords.)

Ask any CEO how s/he feels about the availability of talent. They will say, "There's never enough talent for our needs."

Talent acquisition and the shortage of talent is a global problem, and not only because job descriptions are so often fanciful-bordering-on-delusional.

It's hard to find employees who are not only smart and plucky but also good communicators, flexible and reliable, full of ideas and fun to work with.

When you're facing a shortage of talent -- not total job applicants, but the proactive and self-directed subset of those applicants who can make a difference for your firm and its customers -- is your first thought "Let me make the job application process as off-putting as possible?"

Not if you understand Thing One about human motivation, it's not!

So why has Applicant Tracking System technology changed so little over the years?

Why do we stick with the tired 1980s technology even when we know candidates hate it, and candidates are the only reason we get to make new hires at all?

We stick with an outdated recruiting paradigm, process and technological solution because it is very hard for us to tell the truth about what is broken.

It's hard for us as employers to acknowledge that very often our recruiting processes help us identify the most docile and obedient candidates, rather than the sharpest or most competent ones.

It would be hard on our egos for us to acknowledge that truth, so we don't.

Any employer's recruiting priority is to get great people into the talent pipeline and keep them there.

And what says, "We love you!" more than forty pages of fields that must be filled in, boxes to check, and mind-numbing tedium just to fill out a job application?

When the terse auto-responder shoots back a snippy "Your application has been received (passive voice!) -- if there is interest in your background for any position, we will let you know," talented job seekers with other options -- the very people we should be wooing - conclude that their bread is best buttered elsewhere, and bail.

Can we blame them?

Applicant tracking systems are Black Holes for job seekers.

A candidate lobs a resume in, and nothing comes back. If they are lucky enough to get a response, it's likely to be a different (but still terse) auto-response demanding that they complete an aptitude test or an honesty test.

The honesty tests most employers use are actually intelligence tests, because if you're not smart enough to figure out the 'right' answer on those things ("If you saw an employee stealing, what would you do?") you're not smart enough to have a job.

That being said, online "honesty" tests are insulting and foolish and a waste of time and money.

I've been in HR since 1984, and I have never seen the state of corporate and institutional recruiting at a lower point than where it is today.

We treat job applicants badly at every stage of the process.

We drive them away when we should be welcoming them into our corral.

There's no business justification for it, and our shareholders should be up in arms.

Maybe they've drunk the toxic lemonade that says, "It can't be helped -- there are so many job applicants, we need a mechanical system to sort them all out."

That's not true. We can market to candidates as thoughtfully and narrowly as we market to customers. Marketers learn in a flash that when you market to the wrong people, it costs your company money in the qualification process. It wastes time, and it hurts your brand.

That goes double for recruiting! When you focus on "weeding out" instead of "inviting in," you lose the best candidates, waste precious time and trash your employer brand.

We can be smarter than that. We can evolve past Black Hole recruiting to treat each job seeker like the valued collaborator they is. Our customers need us to figure out how, and so do our shareholders, and so do our communities.

An ATS oriented toward engaging job seekers rather than intimidating and repelling them would be a good start. Once we make contact with a job seeker, that contact should be human.

It isn't complicated to do, but it takes a shift in perspective. In the mid-nineties without benefit of ATS technology (which is nothing more than big, dumb database technology anyway) we hired two or three hundred people a month without difficulty in our growing tech firm.

Any organization can do the same thing, but to humanize a recruiting process you first have to think like a human.

NINE WAYS EMPLOYERS
SCREW UP HIRING

It's a big deal to invite a person to join your team. I understand why a lot of department managers make hiring decisions very carefully. I do the same thing myself.

That being said, almost every part of the traditional corporate and institutional hiring process is sub-optimal and needs attention immediately.

In other parts of our businesses we pay careful attention to processes. We continually tweak and improve them.

What is our goal? We want to make our processes optimal. We talk about usability. What is usability? It means that processes should be easy for humans to understand and to follow. The easier a process is for a normal human being to navigate, the more usable it is.

We stress and obsess about usability when it comes to customers navigating our websites. We hire consultants to assess our customer experiences and tell us where they could be slipperier and faster. Why aren't we doing the same thing with respect our job candidates' experiences?

If you have not looked at your recruiting process from the candidate's point of view lately, now is a great time to dive into that exercise.

If we lose a talented candidate because our hiring practices are too obnoxious, where does that talented person go? They may go and help our competitors beat us in the marketplace!

Here are nine ways employers botch hiring, from the beginning of the recruiting process to the end. Do you have any of these broken processes gumming up your new-hire process?

Hiring Philosophy

Hiring is a critical business function that is tied directly to your organization's mission, so it is important for every organization to have a clear and consistent hiring philosophy that every manager and everyone else involved in the hiring process understands.

You want your team members to be intellectually curious, diverse, eager to learn, supportive of their teammates and confident enough to tell you when you're ticking them off. Or do you want those things? Every organization and leadership team looks for different things in their new hires.

What does your organization look for? A frank discussion of your hiring philosophy might clarify your requirements and preferences.

Most organizations don't have a hiring philosophy, though. Every manager makes up their own hiring philosophy, sometimes on the spot!

Some managers hire people who talk and think the way they do. Some managers hire the people who have the loftiest degrees. Other people hire candidates based on their own fanciful criteria, like the candidates' answers to goofy job-interview questions that have no relationship whatsoever to the job.

We have a lot of work to do to bring up the level of professionalism, not to mention compassion and warmth, in our hiring practices. Creating a company-wide and well-understood hiring philosophy is a great first step to take.

Job Ads

Job ads today still read the way job ads in print newspapers used to read in the nineteen-sixties.

They are dry as dust and terribly off-putting to prospective candidates.

Sometimes job ads are downright insulting! Why would we ever use the third person in a job ad, saying "The Selected Candidate will possess these qualifications...." thereby making it clear to every single reader of the job ad that they is not the *Selected Candidate* we seek?

That's bad marketing, and a job ad is a marketing message.

We need to start selling to our candidates in our job ads, not pushing them away by using our job ads to list all the reasons they're probably not qualified to work for us.

Screening Process

Many, many articles have been written -- a lot of them by me -- about the dismal state of resume screening. Applicant tracking systems are great tools for keeping track of the applicants in your database, and that's all.

It is not a job seeker's job to spend an hour or two populating your candidate database. Do you make your customers populate your customer database? Of course not, because you value your customers. If you don't value job seekers as highly as you value your customers, you will never attract the best people to work for you.

Keyword searching is the worst way ever devised to screen candidates in or out of your process. If you have so many applicants for your job openings that you can't physically look at each person's application or resume, then your recruiting marketing is the problem. Your goal is to market to a small audience of prospective employees, not to splash your job ads against every available surface.

Candidate Communication

Once you hear from a prospective job candidate, your job is to close the loop fast and get that candidate in front of someone in your shop who can make a hiring decision.

Every day that elapses after a candidate contacts you in response to a job ad and before you contact them is a black mark on your company name. If your managers aren't giving their recruiting responsibilities the time and attention they need, they obviously don't care about filling their job vacancies as much as they may have thought they did.

Managers who can't make recruiting one of their top two priorities don't deserve the time and attention of the HR and internal recruiting staff members who are trying to help them recruit. Smart employers have already gotten the memo: candidate communication is the number one recruiting priority for any company that values talent.

Timing

How long should it take you to respond to a candidate at each point in the hiring process? Here are the standards we recommend:

- When a candidate replies to your job ad, they should hear from a human being (not an auto-response email) within three business days.

- Once you've made email contact with a candidate and said you'll get back to them, you've got four business days to do so.

- After a telephone or face-to-face interview, you've got four more business days to let each candidate know their status and the next steps.

- At the final states of the hiring process, when you're close to extending a job offer or once you've made the job offer, someone in HR must be available to talk or correspond with your soon-to-be-new-team-members at all times. No candidate in that stage of the process should wait more than 24 hours to hear back from you when they have a question or a request. Ask yourself this: how long do we make our customers wait to hear back from us?

These are just guidelines, of course. When you train your recruiting eye on hiring marketable candidates with multiple other options, you will find that many of them will not wait as long as the times we recommend above. You have to be on your game to hire amazing candidates but it is WORTH IT.

Accountability

Along with the lack of cohesive recruiting philosophy, a fundamental problem many or most employers face is that the accountability for the success of their recruiting efforts lies with no one.

Most organizations don't have a senior-level person responsible for ensuring that their recruiting practices are top-notch and that the roadblocks I've listed in this column are not gumming up the works.

HR people say, "Hiring managers are too slow to get back to us and tell us which candidates they like." Hiring managers say, "HR isn't giving me good people." Nobody owns the process. That's a recipe for disaster!

Every organization has an annual budgeting process. Often the CFO or someone else in Finance owns that process, which involves every department. It's not only a project management task but a cultural one, too. There is a culture around budgeting in every organization and that culture varies from firm to firm.

There is a unique recruiting culture in every organization, too. Our job as recruiters is to propagate and reinforce that culture and to help new leaders understand the importance of recruiting to them personally and the organization overall. We are evangelists for talent. That's not a process thing – it's a philosophical and emotional journey.

If hiring managers are slow to give us feedback after interviews, that's on us. We can't say, "They messed up." We own the process and we need to find ways (like any evangelist must) to spread the gospel, break down barriers and make our recruiting process so fast and friendly we can beat our competitors for talent every time.

Interview Protocol

Some organizations still interview every applicant using the traditional, Mad-Men-era script, including pointless questions like

"What's your greatest weakness?" and "With all the talented candidates, why should we hire you?"

It is past time to modernize and humanize your interviewing protocol. A job interview is a conversation - nothing more.

Smart employers are relaxed and human in their interviewing processes. They know that until we all take off our masks and get down to real conversation about business problems and solutions in every job interview, we are wasting our time and our companies' money.

Vet/Woo Mix

I came up in HR during the era when the recruiting process was viewed as two separate practices cobbled together. The first practice was called Recruiting and the second one was called Selection. From time to time you still see the term "Recruiting and Selection."

Delusional people who live in a bubble convinced themselves and a whole generation of HR people that we could run job ads (that's the Recruitment part) in order to entice little fishes into our net.

Then, at our leisure, we could sort through the fishes in the net (that's the Selection part) using pre-employment tests and writing samples and questionnaires, and by asking our little netted fishes inane and power-unequal interview questions like "What makes you worthy of joining our team?"

In this fantasy scenario, we could continue our Selection process until we found just the little fish we were looking for. This worldview assumed that the fishes would happily stay in the net until our self-indulgent Screening process was done.

That's absurd.

Recruiting and Selection are not two separate processes.

We need to vet and woo every candidate in equal measure simultaneously throughout the hiring process. We can never stop selling and we can never stop evaluating candidates, if we want to make great hires.

Salary Discussion

It is a waste of time for your company and the talented people in your sphere for you to make job applicants guess what your job openings pay. Responsible employers put a pay range right in their job ads. It is unethical and a horrible, outdated recruiting practice to ask candidates what they earn now or what they were earning at their past jobs, even in places where those questions are legal. It is none of our business.

Don't do it yourself, and don't let your third-party recruiters ask candidates for their salary history or current salary information, either. Doing so marks you as a predatory organization that believes candidates must grovel and beg to get a job with you.

You are not about to share your current employees' payroll information with candidates, so why would you expect them to part with their own, private financial data?

Give them the salary range.

Job Offer Process

The last broken part of the traditional recruiting process is the offer extension part. When you know which candidate you want to hire, you can call that person up and say "Jane, we think you are awesome and we're curious about one thing. If we were to make you a job offer which is the direction we're heading in, what would that offer need to have in it in order for you to accept our offer right away and join our team?"

It's a new millennium now. We have left the Machine Age in the past. We're operating in the Knowledge Economy now, and the best job candidates are also the folks with the highest standards. Who could blame them for that? We need to treat our job candidates like gold. You can make small, gradual changes in your recruiting process and mindset to become the employer everybody in your area wants to work for. That's a goal worth pursuing!

FIVE REASONS TO HIRE SOMEONE – AND FIVE REASONS NOT TO

Dear Liz,

I've been a manager for almost two years, but I still struggle with hiring decisions even though I've hired eleven people so far.

I lead a customer service team. I'm happy about the eleven hiring decisions I've made, for the most part.

Eight of my new hires worked out wonderfully and are still here. Two of them washed out in the first few weeks.

The last person struggled very badly in the job, but we got lucky because there was a job opening in another part of the company. "Margaret" moved into another department after six difficult weeks in my department, and she's happy there.

So, I only have two "fails" out of eleven hires, but those two missteps still bug me. Hiring the wrong person is a very expensive and time-consuming mistake.

I have so much on my plate that I can't afford to hire someone who is not going to be able to come up to speed, or who quits right away.

Right now, I'm interviewing for two customer service reps. I have four to five serious candidates, and of those four to five people

I need to choose two people to hire. All of them seem like smart and motivated people.

Some of them have more experience than the rest, but I'm not sure that more experience is necessarily a great barometer for success in this particular role.

What clues or indicators should I be looking for?

Thanks Liz!

Yours,

Rex

Dear Rex,

Many managers wonder "How should I make hiring decisions?" and that's no surprise.

In the vast canon of HR and leadership literature there is very little said about exactly what to look for when you're hiring!

For years the mantra was "Hire for experience" which is useful in some situations but all wrong in other situations. Some people say, "Hire for potential," but how do you gauge a person's potential, exactly?

We all want to hire smart, capable and enthusiastic people, but we also know that a person's success in any job has a lot to do with the environment, and their interaction with it.

We can't always say for sure whether a person will succeed in a new job, regardless of their experience and/or wonderful personality.

Your hiring track record is excellent, so it would be silly to waste your precious time and energy worrying about how to absolutely, positively avoid hiring the wrong person.

There's no way to guarantee that every new hire will work out.

Here are five good reasons to hire someone, and five good reasons not to!

1. Hire the candidate who has already thought through the assignment and has ideas about how they will approach the job. If you ask the question "How would you approach

this assignment?" and one candidate says "I'd want to study your product literature, read your customer service call scripts, shadow one or two of your most experienced reps and get comfortable with your credit and return procedures" that person may be more ready for the opportunity than a candidate who says "I couldn't really say."

2. Hire the person who can tell you clearly how this role fits into their career plan. A person's reason for pursuing one job over another job is an important part of their brand.

3. Hire the candidate who understands their own career story. Some people run their own careers. They can explain every twist and turn in their career history. Other people don't run a thing — they are blown about like a leaf in the wind. They are not driving their own career. Things happen to them — they do not make things happen.

4. Hire the candidate who can tell you one or several stories about how they made a difference or saved the day at a past job or at school. These stories are called Dragon-Slaying Stories™. Hire the person who knows they have personal power, and knows they get to decide how to use it!

5. Hire the person who has already put themselves mentally into the role. How will you know they've done that? By the thoughtful questions they ask!

6. Don't hire the candidate who has not researched the company and has no questions to ask you.

7. Don't hire a candidate who cannot tell you what they've learned in their career so far. Do not hire a person who has the functional skills to do the job or has very similar experience but can't tell you why they're interested in doing the job again.

8. Don't hire anyone who is more concerned with the "box" around the job — the selection of nearby lunch spots, the location of their workstation or the dress code — than they are concerned with the job itself. (Make an exception for an entry-level job whose main appeal is that it is a steppingstone to better jobs.)

9. Don't hire anyone for a customer service job whose anecdotes illustrate a cynical view toward customers in general. It is easy to develop negative feelings toward all of humanity when you answer the phone forty times a day, but that worldview doesn't work very well in a customer service role. Some candidates cannot help rolling their eyes and mocking their past customers as they tell you about their customer service experience.

   Everyone understands how trying a difficult customer can be, but a person with the mindset "Customers stink!" is not your best customer service hire.

10. Finally, don't hire a person who isn't on top of the details during your recruiting process. Of course, you must be on top of the details on your end, too — keeping your commitment to get back to candidates after interviews and so on.

People show you who they are, and you must believe them when they do. If a candidate gives a great interview but then has to be reminded three times to send over their references, for instance, that's a bad sign.

You have made a great start with your first eleven adventures in recruiting. You will learn something new with every new hire, whether the person you hire is a great long-term employee or not. You will get stronger and stronger every time!

All the best to you,
Liz

SIX EASY WAYS TO HUMANIZE YOUR RECRUITING PROCESS

It wouldn't be so hard to fill job openings if our recruiting processes were more human and functional than they are.

HR people are stuck in the middle. Years ago, somebody highly placed in their organizations fell in love with purely technological solutions to the organization's recruiting problems, even though recruiting problems have less to do with technology and more to do with culture, communication and trust.

Here are steps you can take to humanize your recruiting process.

These are good steps to take if you want to put a human element into your recruiting process without dismantling and rebuilding the entire system from scratch.

Spruce Up Your Front Door

Most automated application systems greet a job seeker with a terse and unfriendly welcome message like "Any fields left blank will subject the applicant to automatic disqualification."

Why would we address people who might be our co-workers in such a rude and off-putting way?

With a few keystrokes you can change the language that greets job seekers in your Applicant Tracking System. Try a friendly greeting like this:

"Welcome! Thank for exploring jobs at Acme Explosives. Most people say that it takes them about eight minutes to complete our online application. We're excited to see your job application, but if you need to stop the process at any point, it's no problem. You can save your application and finish it later!"

You can add more friendly and encouraging messages on other ATS pages.

You can thank the candidate by name when they finish the process and include links to other useful pages on your site, like the employee benefits information page or a greeting from your CEO.

You can also make it easy for candidates to reach you before or during the process of completing your application.

What better way to create a great experience for a candidate than to be available to them before they invest the time and energy it takes to finish your application?

De-Robotize Your Acknowledgment

You may use an auto-responder email message to tell a job applicant that you've received their completed application. Your autoresponder gives you another opportunity to be friendly and human. Instead of the awful, bureaucratic passive voice ("Your materials have been received,") you can switch to human speech and send something like this:

Dear Milo,

Thanks for completing your job application for a Night Supervisor position at Acme Explosives. We really appreciate you investing your time and energy in our direction! We review resumes within about a week after we receive them, so we will have an update for you shortly. Thanks again and enjoy your week!

Yours,
Brenda Smith
Acme HR

HR people are reluctant to divulge their names to job seekers, but why? If someone calls you to say "It's been two and a half weeks and I haven't heard anything back about my application" you want to get that call, because it will signal you that something in your process isn't working.

It's time for HR people to step out from behind the veil and be human -- individual humans, with names -- in the recruiting process. It is a branding world. Your brand as an advocate for candidates is a critical part of your organization's employer brand.

Nice to Meet You!

The best recruiting processes, even at large organizations, are built to ensure that the first contact a job applicant receives from the company (after their application acknowledgment) is a human one.

It could be a phone call or an email message. The HR person who reaches out to the job seeker with an interesting resume is not calling to vet or screen the job seeker. The HR person is doing marketing now!

You can't screen people until they are in your pipeline.

You cannot assume that because someone fills out an application on your site, they want to work for you. You have to market to them before you can safely make that assumption.

I hear from HR people and corporate recruiters who tell me "I reach out to people who filled out applications, and they don't respond!" Much of that problem is related to the way we reach out. "Passive candidates" are busy people. If we take up their time, we have to give them a good reason why.

No one gets excited about an email message that says "You may be a match for our Inventory Analyst III position. Please follow the link below to our online Honesty Test, Writing Test and Basic Math test."

We cannot ask job seekers to work for you for free, and even before they've heard from a human being on your staff. If we send people tests to complete and questionnaires to fill out before anyone on our team has spoken to them, the truth is that we don't deserve their talents.

Here's a friendly "Next step" message:

Dear Joseph,

Thanks for your application for the Inventory Analyst position at Acme Explosives. Our team was happy to receive your resume and application. I'd be grateful for the opportunity to talk with you about the position when you have time. I can also answer your questions about the job. Do you have time over the next few days to chat by phone? I'm looking forward to meeting you virtually!

Yours,
Derek Carson
Acme Explosives Recruiting

Interviewing with a Human Voice™

Get rid of the interview script and have a conversation over coffee or tea or kombucha or whatever you like to drink. Whether your interviews are virtual or in-person, they can be friendly and conversational.

In the Interviewing with a Human Voice™ protocol we teach interviewers to give the job candidate the floor, first. You can have a great interview without asking a job seeker even one question.

The quality of the thinking behind your job applicants' questions will tell you much more about them than answers to your scripted questions will. Throw out the interview script, and just talk.

Tell your story and let the person you're meeting tell you theirs. Talk about what a day in the job is like. Talk about what's challenging in the job and where the career path from this position could lead.

Ask the job seeker to brainstorm with you about a problem you're facing in the department right now. You want to see neural activity! You've got to show some neural activity, too. The more human and relaxed the interview can be, the better!

Keep Candidates Warm

Once a job seeker enters a recruiting pipeline, we owe them an update every week at a minimum. When we leave candidates in Radio Silence Land, we signal that they mean nothing to the organization. If our hiring managers are slow getting back to you with feedback after their interviews, we will nudge them to pick up the pace.

Polite persistence pays off. Go to their office. Remind them that live human beings are waiting to hear the results of the hiring manager's decision. We would not shrug our shoulders about a missed deadline that affected our vendors or customers. Alacrity is at least as important in the recruiting process.

More than once I have had to tell a department manager that I would need to put their job openings on hold unless they could respond to me with interview feedback promptly after each interview.

That's more than reasonable. Your time is a limited resource and must be spent working on vacancies that the department manager has a real interest in filling, and soon.

Celebrations and Thanks

Make a Supposal to your top candidate before extending an offer, as it's rude and a waste of everyone's time to present a candidate with a job offer whose contents are a mystery to them until they receive it.

Walk through the offer in a Supposal conversation and only create a written offer letter when you and your job candidate have agreed on everything the letter will contain.

Here's how that looks: "Sally, we are getting close to potentially extending an offer, so I wanted to check in with you. Supposing we offered you this salary and this title, would that work for you?"

It's stressful to make the decision to take a new job, even when you really need a job! You can support the candidate by being on hand to answer their questions and making sure they have all the new-arrival information they need.

When you call or write to the candidates who didn't get the job, use the same gracious manners you employ with your new employees. Everyone is a friend, whether you hire them right now or not.

Every step in the recruiting process can be warm, friendly and professional. It doesn't need to be harsh and formal. We don't hire better employees when our recruiting processes are stiff and impersonal. In fact, our inhuman recruiting processes are a big part of the reason we have as much trouble filling jobs as we do!

That's okay. Every step we take to humanize our recruiting process pays off magnificently.

Investing a little time and energy to warm up your recruiting process is one of the most important things you can do to help your organization compete and thrive. What other HR priority takes precedence over that?

DON'T HIRE THAT CHANGE AGENT!

I can understand an executive's temptation to hire a shake-em-up Change Agent when big changes need to happen in an organization. But haven't we learned through harsh experience that this strategy backfires 99 percent of the time?

Leaders too often hire Change Agents—charismatic people with blue-chip Change Management and Project Management credentials and backbones of steel (we hope)—and watch them fail within a year.

The patron saint of Change Agents could only be Saint Sebastian, whose portraits always show him pierced by arrows. In fact, people say, "You can always spot a Change Agent by the arrows in their back."

What is it about the Change Agent approach that causes things to go so badly, so often?

Here's the first question for an executive to ask: "If I care so much about change, why haven't I changed things around here myself?"

CEOs and vice presidents talk themselves into believing that the reason they have not driven the organizational transformation they seek is that they've been too busy with other things.

A leader whose reason for hiring a Change Agent is time-related is a leader who would rather talk about change than experience it. The truth is that if the executive wanted things to be different, they would be different right now, long before the Change Agent hits the scene.

The second common excuse is that change happens far down in the organization, on teams the executives have little contact with.

That sounds nice, but it's unconvincing in real life because the people on those teams take orders from people two or three levels higher in the organization. When change is a corporate priority, the CEO and everyone else is talking about it. It isn't just an issue for the rank-and-file workers.

The very notion of a designated person to drive change is pathetic because real change in organizations isn't one person's job and doesn't happen under the guidance of any one executive—even the CEO.

When change is a real priority, it's the central topic in every staff meeting. It's the No. 1 item against which leaders are evaluated, and the CEO and her team are singing about it from the rafters.

When the change is more lip service than conviction, a handy (and handily dispensable) Change Agent might help an uncommitted-to-change executive feel as though they're trying to do something useful without putting their own career at risk.

We know better. When change is a corporate imperative, senior executives will be driving change themselves, and everyone in the joint will act as a Change Agent, in one way or another.

HOW TO SPEAK UP AT WORK --
WHEN EVERYONE ELSE IS SILENT

Dear Liz,

I like my job about 80% of the time, but the other 20% of the time I hate it.

I manage events for a national association. The problem is that when my boss "Rachel" gets stressed, she becomes abusive to me and my co-workers. Everyone in the department is afraid of her.

Sometimes really bad ideas come down from upper management and Rachel has to implement them. She stomps around and gets mad at us for no reason when she has to carry out a dumb idea from senior management. She knows these ideas are terrible, but she's afraid to tell her boss how she feels.

We tell her "Rachel, you can tell the higher-up managers why their idea isn't workable. You would be doing them a favor if you were honest with them. You don't have to keep your mouth shut."

Rachel is way too fearful to speak up about misguided ideas she is expected to put into place.

I'm not afraid. I don't care if a higher-up manager gets bent out of shape when I say, "Here's a better way to accomplish your goal."

I can get another job if I lose this one, and anyway the higher-up managers like me because I put on great events that make our association a lot of money. I'm pretty sure they would listen to me.

Should I go to our VP myself, and leave Rachel out of it? I'm sick of trying to coach her to stand up for herself (and stand up for our department) when time after time, she won't or can't do it.

At our staff meetings, nobody has the nerve to tell Rachel the truth. Last month I wanted to say "Remember when you forced us to implement that change in the membership policies last month? Well, the members hate it and we've had over 300 complaints come in."

I didn't do it because I didn't want to make Rachel mad in the meeting where she might take out her frustration on our department.

I stay silent because I don't want to be the one to create conflict, and my co-workers stay silent because they're afraid of Rachel. The air is so thick you can feel the tension in the room, but nobody says a word.

What should I do?

Thanks Liz! You are my HR guru -

Yours,
Natalie

Dear Natalie,

The question to ponder in a situation like yours isn't "How do I speak up?" but rather "What do I want to bring about, and what is the best way to do that?"

If you want to take on the project of helping Rachel find her voice with the higher-up managers, the best way to do it is probably not by discussing failed policies in a public setting like a staff meeting.

The best way to coach anyone is one-on-one, in a low-stress setting. It takes time to build the trust between you and your manager that would allow them to be honest with you about their fears and concerns.

You will need to cultivate so much trust between you and Rachel that she tells you "I'm frustrated about these dumb policy changes that I'm expected to implement."

You will begin coaching Rachel by asking her the same questions I'm asking you: What would you like to bring about? How would you like to see the situation change? What are you willing to do, to achieve that result?

Rachel might say "I want my managers to stop giving me goofy plans to implement."

Then you'd ask her to think about what would have to change for that goal to become reality. The answer — obvious to you, but not to Rachel in her fearful state — might be that Rachel would need to find her voice and educate her managers about the real state of things on the ground.

Over time, Rachel may confess to you that she's afraid to speak up. Then you can talk to her about the costs and benefits — to her and the whole organization — of her silence.

If you go directly to your VP to explain why some of their ideas aren't working out, you may shift their thinking. That would be good for you, your members and the VP, but it wouldn't help Rachel a bit. You need to ask yourself: what is my mission here?

Maybe your mission is to build new muscles coaching Rachel to step out of her fear. Maybe your mission is to grow your own muscles by using your voice and your backbone.

Maybe your mission is to take your talents to a place that isn't so fraught and tense, and let your light shine as brightly as it wants to!

This is a time for reflection. When you feel your power coursing in your veins, it's easy to speak up. At the same time, if the people above you at work can't hear what you are trying to tell them, why do they still deserve your time and talents?

When I was younger, I was the designated Speak Up person at almost every meeting. Over time I learned that I wasn't helping anybody by bringing up all the spicy and sticky topics while everybody else stayed quiet.

Eventually I realized that I made it easy for my co-workers to stay quiet because they knew I would speak for them.

They started to bring me issues and say "Can you please bring up this topic at our meeting? I'm afraid to — but you're not!"

If you are the only person willing to talk about workplace topics that desperately need airtime, you are not in the right place.

Is it your job to single-handedly shift your culture out of fear and into trust? I doubt it. Maybe Mother Nature is nudging you to consider a change of venue.

Only the people who get you, deserve you after all!

All the best,
Liz

'INDUSTRY EXPERIENCE' IS OVERRATED -- AND EVERYBODY KNOWS IT

You only have to work in a couple of different white-collar jobs to see how interchangeable white-collar skill sets are.

To be successful in a white-collar job, you have to be able to talk to people, and you have to be able to solve problems by yourself and in groups.

You have to be able to read and hear things and integrate them into your thinking, and you must be able to follow a project plan or build your own project plan and follow it.

White-collar jobs fall across a spectrum regarding the importance of subject-matter expertise to success in the job.

In some jobs, you must have twenty or thirty years of very specific experience in order to perform the job, but it is many more situations you can walk into a job and pick up the industry jargon and concepts once you are there.

Over time as you work at a succession of different jobs, you see just how similar all white-collar jobs are to one another. The similarities between jobs vastly outnumber the differences!

In the business and professional worlds, we convince ourselves that industry-specific experience and functional subject-matter expertise are tremendously important in jobs where they simply are not.

We lie to ourselves and one another about the necessity of industry experience.

If you leave out technical, legal, military, medical and some (not all) financial positions almost any bright and capable person can pick up any white-collar job in months rather than years.

White-collar work does not often involve rocket science, but we have incentives to pretend that it does -- that our jobs could never be performed by anyone who doesn't have a deep and comprehensive functional or industry background.

If our industry experience isn't terribly valuable, we might not be as lofty and impressive as we want to be!

If Joe Blow with no industry experience whatsoever could waltz in from some other industry and do your job, then your already shaky job security might evaporate altogether.

For years I have heard "the world wants specialists, not generalists," but that is not true. The world desperately needs non-specialists and broad thinkers. It's just that too often, we have been trained to write job ads as though only specialized knowledge could possibly be useful in the job.

Industry experience can just as often be a hindrance as a help to a new employee -- much less to their employer!

Groupthink is a real problem in business -- one of the biggest problems businesses face.

We don't see it as a problem or address it as a threat only because it is so comforting to have our most strongly held beliefs reinforced by the people around us.

We need outsiders to come in from wildly different industries and functions and point out the things that are obvious to them but invisible to us.

I had no background in HR when I became an HR manager. I had the outsider's advantage. I had the same glasses on that you have when you're on a vacation in a strange place.

I got to observe HR from an outsider's perspective. I saw the incredible opportunity my teammates and I had to build a talent-attracting, people-first culture that would power our organization to massive growth.

I also saw how HR and leadership done badly kill an organization's hopes to hire or keep great employees, customers or chances at success.

Fear-based management was going strong in the nineteen-eighties, and the problem has only gotten worse since then.

The obsession with industry experience in a recruiting process is a testament to a bureaucratic mindset and culture.

If you care about building your business and bobbing and weaving in concert with the fast-changing world, you will hire people with radically different experiences than your own.

You will leap far across the universe of functions and industries to hire people who will challenge your view of the world.

You will hire people who have made life and career choices you would never make.

Your non-traditionally experienced, truth-telling teammates will give you perspectives you would never dream up on your own.

You will step into your leadership power and open yourself and your business to possibilities you cannot see right now. That's true leadership.

Are you ready to step out of an old box and invite fresh viewpoints into your company, and your mind?

TEN THINGS I LOOK FOR WHEN I'M HIRING

I couldn't care less whether someone I am considering for a job opening has done the job before. If they've already done the job, my first question will be "Why do you want to do the same thing again?" I want to understand a job seeker's path. Where are they headed?

That doesn't mean that I expect or want someone to have a five-year plan. I certainly don't have a five-year plan. Five years is a long time. Why would I try to box in Mother Nature?

I have a vision that I'm working toward -- but I wouldn't ask a job applicant, "What's your vision for yourself?" That's a personal question. I only need to know why this job makes sense for you, apart from the fact that you need a job.

I ran a job ad for an Editor one time and got 150 responses. In the job ad I said, "In your email response please share two or three reactions to our latest newsletter," and I included the link to our newsletter.

Of the 150 or so responses, 40 people included comments on the newsletter, and the vast majority of those reactions were "It's a nice newsletter."

Ten people shared thoughtful comments on our newsletter, and we interviewed those ten folks. One of them got the job.

Of the ten people we interviewed for the Editor position, only two people had had Editor titles before. One person was a stage manager and another one had been working in Finance but burned out on it. Past experience in many areas (not all!) is overrated.

"Industry experience" is a particularly unfortunate requirement, because having spent time in different industries is a good thing, not a bad thing!

Most intellectually curious adults can perform most white-collar jobs, if we are honest. If we hired people based on their brains and pluck instead of the words on their resume, we'd make better hires, faster, and get better results, but we are afraid to take a chance on a person.

That's crazy, but there is a lot of fear in the working world.

Most of the nonsense that job seekers must put up regarding their Job Qualifications is based on the fiction that you have to have done a job already in order to get the job.

It makes no sense!

Here are the 10 things I look for when I'm hiring people:

1. I look for someone who is curious.

2. I look for someone who is game -- who has tried things just for the heck of it and has taken risks.

3. I look for someone who's confident.

4. I look for someone who can communicate their thoughts clearly, and who has opinions.

5. I look for someone who speaks their mind.

6. I look for someone who has taken the time to investigate our organization and think about it.

7. I look for someone who is looking to learn and can tell me a few important things they have already learned.

8. I look for someone with a sense of humor.

9. I look for someone who is reliable and ethical.

10. Lastly, I look for someone who isn't afraid of me, managers in general or anyone else.

TEN THINGS YOUR RESUME DOESN'T MENTION -- BUT IT SHOULD

For fifty or sixty years, job candidates have been taught to write their resumes in the most opaque and unhelpful way imaginable.

They have been taught to use terse, governmental language in their resumes, so that almost every job seeker sounds identical to every other job seeker!

That's the worst possible approach. You are not a dry, dusty person — you are lively and creative! Why not show some of that creativity and spark in your resume?

These days we need to tell our story in a resume, but traditional resume-writing rules say nothing about your story. That's a shame, because your story is your brand!

Your path in life is one of the most critical things anyone could hope to know about you — but it's almost entirely missing from a traditional resume.

Here are 10 things your resume needs to convey if you want it to sing your song effectively:

1. Why you changed jobs each time you did

2. How you see yourself in your career (how you are different from other people with similar career paths)

3. Why you chose the career path you did

4. Why you were brought on board at each job

5. What you left in your wake at each job

6. Your personality and sense of humor

7. The context for each of your triumphs

8. Your priorities in your job

9. What you accumulated experience-wise at each job you've held, and

10. How your brain works

None of this is typically taught to job seekers, but all of it is critical!

Here are two excerpts from Miranda's Human-Voiced Resume™ that illustrate these essential elements.

Here is the Summary at the top of Miranda's resume:

I'm a Product Manager in the construction industry, focused on revenue and product cost. I thrive when I can work closely with product developers, suppliers and my Sales and Manufacturing colleagues to make sure every product I launch leads the industry and finds it audience fast.

What has Miranda told us so far? We see that she is not afraid to use her human voice, for one thing.

If somebody turns up their nose at Miranda's full sentences and her use of the word "I," she's fine with that. Miranda know that not everybody deserves her talents!

Miranda tells us plainly what she intends to do in her next job. We see that Miranda is driven and down to earth.

Here is another excerpt from Miranda's Human-Voiced Resume™. This time, she describes her tenure at Acme Explosives.

Acme Explosives, Inc., Fayetteville, Arkansas
Product Manager
2009 — 2014

Acme is a $10M family-owned stick dynamite manufacturer. I was hired to establish the company's first product management function and to launch the world's first modular (and thus shippable) stick dynamite product.

- In my first year I built the Product Management team and department, launched the X-15 modular product and revamped two older product lines.

- The products we launched generated $5M in sales, doubling the company's revenue

- I left Acme after its acquisition by Toontown Industries

Miranda covered several of our ten essential elements in her description of her time at Acme Explosives:

1. In her third and final bullet, she tells us why she left the firm — something every hiring manager wants to know!

2. In her initial framing statement, she tells us what Acme Explosives is all about and how large a company they are — and why she was brought on board to help them.

3. Miranda gives us the context for her accomplishments and tells us what she left in her wake at Acme Explosives. This is far more relevant and useful to a hiring decision-maker than a list of the tasks and duties any Product Manager would have performed!

4. Finally, Miranda is opening her brain so we can see how it works. We know already that Miranda is very focused on revenue — a good thing for a Product Manager to be!

You can do the same thing Miranda did. You can convey a lot more information in your one-or-two-page resume than most job seekers do!

NO, I WON'T BUILD YOUR WEBSITE 'AS PART OF THE INTERVIEW PROCESS'

Dear Liz,

I just interviewed with an up-and-coming consulting business that has grown from four people to 60 employees in less than a year.

That's impressive, but it doesn't mean they know what they're doing. I don't know whether this company will have 150 employees a year from now or be down to ten people.

I asked a lot of questions, but they didn't tell me much about the inner workings of the business.

However, they asked me incredibly detailed questions about how I design websites — the kind of questions that make me think they want to steal my ideas instead of hiring me.

After three interviews, they asked me to build a "small" website for them, just to show them what I'm capable of.

I was disappointed because I didn't expect them to be so tacky, but I was also glad they showed me their true colors before I started working for them.

I told them I'd be happy to design their "small" website for a small fee.

They said "Sure, sure, of course!" and then they said "We have a few other people we're talking to — and some of them are a lot more experienced than you are," and that was the end of that. I won't hear from them again.

Interestingly, the same day I got the "free website" request, a friend of my girlfriend's ex-roommate learned that two employees of the up-and-coming consulting firm had asked their client if they could come and work for the client company.

They want to get out of the consulting firm.

My girlfriend's ex-roommate's friend knew one of the two women who wanted to leave the consulting firm. The two women had only worked for the consulting firm for six weeks, but that was long enough.

They had not received a paycheck in six weeks even though they were told the payroll is processed every two weeks. The consulting firm had been making excuses for four weeks!

I don't know what happened to those two women, but I know I dodged a bullet. Thanks for reminding us that we have more power than we think!

Yours,

Dear Elias,

The people who asked you to design a website for free would never dream of calling a plumbing company and saying "Can you send over a plumber to do a little plumbing work in my house for free — just so I can evaluate their work?"

It takes chutzpah to ask someone to work for free! I doubt that the consulting firm would offer to do a little consulting work for free. I hope those two women eventually get paid. They can file a complaint with their state's labor department if they don't.

Even though you must feel like you wasted time with those folks, you were growing muscles all the while. You found your voice to say "Why no, I sure won't design a free website for you — best of luck with that project!" and that's a big accomplishment.

I'm sure you know that some desperate job seekers would have designed the website for free, and then they would really have felt bad when they still didn't get the job.

A friend of mine worked for a resume-writing agency back in the 1980s. The resume-writing agency's owner was so cheap and unprofessional that he made his resume writers call up various office copier vendors and have them install copiers in the office on a trial basis, to check out the copier's speed and features.

I guess that back then, copier companies would do that. They would install a copier in your office if you asked them to. After thirty or sixty days you had to pay for the copier or return it.

The resume-writing agency owner would use the free copier for thirty or sixty days and then return it, and then ask another vendor for another free copier.

There were enough vendors that the guy was able to keep his business running by using free copiers and constantly switching them in and out. What we can do about people like that?

We can learn to spot them early in the game, and avoid them!

The more toads and other reptiles you come across, the stronger your spidey sense will become!

All the best to you,
Liz

RECRUITING ISN'T HARD -- WE MAKE IT HARD

We make recruiting harder than it needs to be.

I ran a Fortune 500 HR team. How did we hire thousands of people? We had amazing managers and HR people, for one thing. We had tremendous employees in every department who brought their friends to work and got paid for it and got other benefits.

I remember maybe six incidents of really off-the-wall issues with employees over a decade. We were very lucky in that respect, but it was the kind of luck you make yourself when you make a workplace human. Any company can do it.

If there was a disturbance in the Force in any division or team, somebody who could fix it would hear about it fast. There's no HR program that creates those connections and relationships. They come from trust. You build trust slowly, and you begin that project by taking down the barriers that tell your team members "Don't trust us, because as you can see, we don't trust you!"

The barriers are excess policies, insulting rules, hierarchy, fear and control. You probably have some of that in your organization. That's where you can start -- you can talk about those things and begin breaking them down.

If you ever broke down a stage set after the closing night of the show, you know what it's like to dismantle a construction project piece by piece. That's what you'll do. You'll get rid of half the policies in your policy manual and re-write the rest of them to take the robotic, bureaucratic corporate voice out.

You'll gradually soften and humanize your culture. It will be a lot of fun to do it! Your recruiting will get easier. You'll get rid of half the Essential Requirements in your job ads. You'll interview people with an eye toward who they are and where they've been, not how many certifications they have.

You'll treat your job candidates like gold and make a hiring decision quickly. You'll stay in touch with the people you don't hire. You'll make new fans for your company in the process. Every new hire will be easier than the last because the cultural pixie dust will already be out in your recruiting ecosystem.

You'll start by dropping a stone into the water and watching the ripples get bigger. You can start today!

We started to teach Recruiting with a Human Voice™ because everywhere we looked HR people were saying "It's so hard to fill these job openings!"

How can that be? We control our recruiting process, our salary structure and every other aspect of recruiting.

All we have to do to compete effectively in the talent market is to be kinder, warmer, more authentic, more responsive and more tuned in to candidates' needs than other firms.

That's a challenge worth stepping up to!

In many or most medium-sized and large employers, the recruiting processes are in desperate need of an overhaul. They are frustrating not only for candidates but for hiring managers and the HR and Recruiting teams that administer them.

In Marketing we say "Staple yourself to an order. See if you can replicate the experience your customer has when they places an order with your company."

That's a good exercise. We can do the same thing in recruiting. We can take the candidate's point of view and see how our own recruiting practices are driving talented people away -- people who could help us solve our thorniest business problems.

Ask your Applicant Tracking System vendor how you can check on the abandonment rate of your candidates. Ecommerce marketers lose sleep over their shopping cart abandonment rates, and we should be just as tuned in to the abandonment rate of visitors to our companies' career sites.

If people begin your job-application process and drop out halfway through, they've cast their vote. They don't feel that whatever is waiting for them behind the veil is worth the time and effort they'll have to put into it. That's not an irrational reaction.

It's appropriate for people to invest their time and energy wisely -- I hope you do! If we don't sell job candidates effectively enough to fill our open positions quickly, that's on us.

No one else bears any responsibility for that -- no college placement service, no recruiter, and no job seeker. You know what they say: "When your customer doesn't buy from you, s/he made the right decision."

We have to learn to sell our companies to job seekers and sell our opportunities. We're not all that good at selling, because for years we thought our jobs as HR folks and internal recruiters was to screen people out. That's okay! We can become amazing salespeople. It's not hard. It just takes a shift in our perspective.

When someone bails on your application process, it's because they don't care enough about whatever job you might have open to finish the process. Why? It's probably because your process is tedious and insulting.

Why not change your recruiting process to make it simple and fun? You can make your entire recruiting process faster and more polite at the same time. You'll get better candidates, and the new hire process will cost you less than it does now.

It takes time but not necessarily any cash to make your recruiting process nimbler and more candidate friendly. You can make small changes that will have big positive effect.

That is satisfying for you as well as every recruiter or HR person, department manager and candidate in your talent acquisition world.

We tell ourselves that smart and capable people will spend hours sitting at a keyboard completing clerical tasks for our convenience, filling out field after field in an unfriendly and rigid Applicant Tracking System. The trouble is that the more marketable a candidate is, the less willing they are to plow through the submission process.

We cannot really blame them. If we want to hire talented people, shouldn't we welcome them in rather than pushing them away?

Your recruiting becomes faster and easier when you make it a lively and organic process. You'll make new hires more quickly and everyone involved will feel better about the process, including the folks who don't get the job.

Everything your business needs -- new ideas, passion, ambitious projects and "Ahas!' from the outside world -- comes from hiring terrific people. It is the most compelling, easy-to-acquire and sustainable competitive advantage there is, to hire and keep great employees.

What is competitive advantage made of? Competitive advantages come from one thing: responsiveness to your market. Competitive advantage of any kind relies on your ability to listen to reality and align with it.

It is no different in the recruiting realm.

We can change every piece of the recruiting process by shifting our view to see that recruiting is a sales and marketing activity. We are selling job seekers on working with us. How do we sell our customers? We do it by valuing them from the first contact and asking them questions and listening to their answers.

We can do the same thing in recruiting – and let the results speak for themselves.

FIXING THE RECRUITING PROCESS IN FIVE EASY STEPS

If a CEO or CHRO were inclined to re-design their organization's recruiting process to make it work for people, here are five ways they could go about it:

Add a reality requirement to job requisitions

It's bad to see job requisitions that require applicants to hold three specific degrees and eight certifications, have twenty years of experience in ten-year-old technologies, and also have superpowers. It's worse when the imaginary job candidate is expected to bring all these assets to a firm for a low wage.

If you want your recruiting process to make sense, reality-check your job requisitions before they can be posted. Beyond the critical few job requirements, every other 'nice to have' bullet point would cost the hiring manager in budget dollars. After all, the more skills we demand, the more expensive the search will be and the longer it will take.

Consider internal candidates and friends-of-employees first

The outside candidate who goes through several interviews only to hear, "You know, we also have an internal candidate" is a person with a very good reason for being ticked off.

It's only responsible for an employer to look at internal candidates first, before wasting anyone else's time. After internal candidates, we should be telling our employees (and vendors, customers and friends) about our job openings so they can let their friends know.

Only after those channels have been exhausted should we put our job openings out for public display. Where are the Process Quality folks when we need them?

Make sure your Diversity recruiting program is in good shape before relying heavily on employee referrals. Of course, broadening your pool of talent is a good objective at any time, no matter how diverse your team may be already.

Mandate that the requisition expires in 30 days

If a manager needs help, they should make recruiting a top priority.

Yet job candidates sit waiting while processes creak forward, then stop, then lurch forward again. That's hard on HR people and recruiters, as well as candidate.

If a hiring manager, aided by a competent recruiting partner, can't fill a job in 30 days, then it may be the case that the job requirements are unrealistic.

Instead of turning over every rock on the beach, we can simplify the job spec so that a bigger pool of candidates could fill the role.

Any job opening that has been marketed for over thirty days without turning up reasonable candidates is a job spec with a problem. Rather than continuing to run ads and interview people only for the hiring manager to say, "No, thanks" to each of them, the thirty-day mark is a great time for a more serious conversation.

Why is this job so hard to fill? Is the job description unappealing? Does the job pay enough? Are we asking for too many requirements, and obscure requirements at that?

Are candidates dropping out of our pipeline and if so, why?

Don't let a job opening sit unexamined once it hits the thirty-day point. Jump on it and make adjustments or decide to put the job opening on hold while you sort things out.

Focus on the first forty-eight

If you want to boost the quality of your hires and your organization's overall leadership quotient, make a rule that every job candidate brought in for an interview needs a yes or no message within 48 hours after their interview - no exceptions.

That will get your managers thinking about timeliness in the recruiting system. If the manager hasn't checked in with the candidate by the 48-hour mark, that candidate will be handed to another hiring manager in the company while the slowpoke manager gets to go find new contenders. If you snooze, you lose, right?

Install quality in hiring metrics

We evaluate HR people on a terrible metric called "Time to Fill'. Once we put in place a thirty-day explosion clause (described above) we can forget about "Time to Fill" and focus on quality in the recruitment and selection processes themselves.

If we want to do this right, we'll ask the job candidates – I'm talking about the people who WEREN'T hired – how well the managers and HR people have done at communicating and answering questions throughout the process. Eye-opening!

We can get much better at managing recruiting now, and waste no time making our recruiting engine a competitive weapon for our organization.

From the language on your careers site to the way you greet interviewees in the lobby, every bit of the process contributes to your message to the marketplace. You want the message to be, "Recruiting amazing employees is the most important thing we do."

TEN RIDICULOUS HR IDEAS THAT NEED TO DIE

Here are 10 ridiculous HR ideas that should have been tossed on the trash heap years ago.

1. Stack ranking/forced ranking programs in which employees are compared to one another and rated "best" to "worst."

2. Annual performance reviews. Planning sessions are great -- but what could possibly be the purpose of reviewing the last year to call out mistakes and missteps -- or worse, of giving an employee a numeric ranking or grade like a little kid in school? Performance reviews are pointless, insulting and culture-killing programs that smart companies are ditching in droves.

3. 360-Degree feedback systems. Who could tell employees with a straight face "We are going to help you perform at a higher level by having your co-workers anonymously supply feedback on your shortcomings -- without attribution, specific details, or any context around the events that led to their assessment."

Real leaders don't make their employees fill out anonymous feedback forms. That's a great way to kill trust on a team -- not build it!

4. Bereavement Leave policies that require an employee to bring in a funeral notice when a loved one dies.

5. The management philosophy that treats attendance as a disciplinary issue -- as though your employees choose to be sick, get injured, have their car break down or experience a basement flood. Don't join any company without reading its attendance policy from beginning to end!

6. The practice of allowing department managers to approve or deny their team members' applications for internal transfers and promotions. This policy is a fear-based manager's dream! Luckily for them and sadly for you, good employees who are thwarted in their ambitions will simply leave your company and join one of your competitors.

7. Watching like a hawk when employees arrive and depart from work but ignoring the hours they spend working overtime or taking work home. If your company is fussy about attendance for salaried employees but doesn't give them credit for working on their own time, the company doesn't deserve them (or you).

8. Prohibiting department managers from giving great references to former employees. Companies are so irrationally afraid of defamation lawsuits that they muzzle their own managers -- the same people they trust to do the daily blocking and tackling that keeps the company going -- when it comes to giving references. How can someone be qualified to run a department but incapable of providing a non-defamatory reference for a former team member? "No-reference" policies do a grave disservice to former employees who may have served your company for years -- and signal to your current teammates that once they

leave your company, the rest of their career is none of your concern.

9. Stealing frequent-flyer miles from your business-traveling employees. When someone's tush is in that airline seat, the stress on their body is real. To steal their miles out of cheapness is to signal to your employees (and by extension, to the whole world) that your company is penny-wise and pound-foolish.

10. The last awful HR idea on our list is the idea that you can hire great people by subjecting them to insulting online application forms and then using a keyword-searching algorithm to screen resumes for you.

It's a new day in the workplace. Smart and capable people are in demand, but only if they know their own value!

PART TWO

THE PROCESS

SHOULD HR FOLKS HELP CANDIDATES WITH THEIR INTERVIEWING SKILLS?

Dear Liz,

I hope you can help me with a disagreement I am having with one of my colleagues.

I'm the local HR rep and recruiter for a branch of my firm. I support two divisions. I do all the recruiting for both divisions. Several weeks ago, we had a regional meeting in our facility. Three other recruiters/HR reps from other regions were here for a week, in meetings.

The meetings were great. At one point we had a break in our meeting schedule, and I had an initial interview to conduct. I asked my colleague "Christopher" (who works in a different location, for a different division) if he wanted to join me in the interview and he said yes.

We interviewed a young woman applying for what would be her second full-time job. We had a good conversation. At one point the applicant, "Samantha," asked me, "What kinds of questions will the hiring manager ask me? Do you have any tips for me?"

I said "That's a great question. The department manager Alex is likely to ask you about your experience, and it's important for you to tell Alex one or two stories that showcase how you made a positive difference at work. Here's an example of a story from my background rather than yours." Then I told a little story.

Out of the corner of my eye I saw my colleague "Christopher" looking horrified. After Samantha left, Chris said "Derek, you don't ever coach job applicants on their interviewing technique! You just don't!"

I said, "Why not?" I was an external recruiter before I took this job, and we always coached our candidates. Why wouldn't you help somebody do their best at an interview, especially when they specifically ask you for your help?

Chris said, "If you don't do that for every employee, it's not fair." I completely disagree. I only answer the questions that job candidates ask me. I don't run down a whole script of possible answers to questions they haven't asked. I agree with you Liz that the questions a candidate asks us are much more important than their answers to any scripted questions.

I thought Samantha's question was great and my advice was only intended to help an otherwise qualified candidate make a better impression at the interview and if appropriate, get the job. I'm supposed to help people do their best — candidates and hiring managers alike.

Do you think it's right or wrong for HR people or recruiters to coach job applicants on their interviewing technique?

Thanks!

Yours,

Dear Derek,

There are two energy fields at work, and they are in constant conflict. The trick to staying human and succeeding in your career is to manage the interplay between the two competing energy fields.

One energy field is made of fear, and the other one is made of trust.

If a CEO doesn't trust their recruiters to be fair and equitable in dealing with candidates, then no process and no rules will assuage that fear.

If a CEO trusts their recruiters to be upright and ethical with every candidate and every manager, they will not worry about a recruiter giving a candidate any unfair advantage over other candidates for the recruiter's own nefarious purposes.

I agree that if a candidate asks for help with their interviewing technique there is no reason whatsoever not to offer your advice.

Sadly, there are organizations that expressly prohibit recruiters and hiring managers from aiding or even encouraging candidates during the interview process.

A few years back I met some HR folks who work for an organization that does not allow its recruiters or other interviewers to smile or nod at job candidates. They are not allowed to seem to encourage the candidate in any way, for example by saying "What an interesting point," or "Great observation."

That is sick. That is literally not healthy. There is no inherent fairness built into saying the exact same things to every candidate in the exact same order or withholding normal human emotions like civility and reinforcement in such a personal and stressful setting as a job interview.

Many people drawn to HR and recruiting roles are naturally "coach" types. It is instinctive for them to encourage job candidates and everyone else they spend time with. Who would tell them not to?

That goofy "no encouragement of candidates" rule comes straight out of the Fear-Based Management Handbook.

In fact, to ask a person to bite their tongue rather than say "Great answer!" or suppress a smile or a nod is a form of workplace abuse. It requires a working person to shut down their personality, and that is unethical at its core.

It sounds like this topic would inspire a great group discussion at your next regional meeting.

In the meantime, talk to your boss and the leaders of the divisions you support. Ask them how they feel about the question "Is it okay for me to help job applicants do a better job at their interviews, since my role is to hire great people to fuel the company's growth?"

I can't wait to hear what they say!

All the best,
Liz

TEN THINGS GOOD RECRUITERS DO (AND BAD ONES DON'T)

We must run our careers like entrepreneurs now. We must be choosy about the employers we work for, because working in the wrong job can hurt your resume and damage your confidence badly, too!

Allowing yourself to be represented to employers by the wrong recruiter is another bad move.

Choose your recruiters carefully!

The recruiter is a talent scout. You are the talent. It's your career, and it's your life. You get to decide who has your resume.

Here are ten things all good recruiters do -- and bad ones do not.

Good recruiters sell you before they quiz you

Good recruiters sell you on working with them, not by droning on about how many excellent candidates they've placed into jobs, but by asking you what you want next in your career and listening to your answers.

They sell you on working with them the same way any good salesperson sells a customer.

They don't talk over you. They don't cut you off in mid-sentence. If a recruiter does those things, flee! That is not the person to be your representative.

The recruiter is going to need to hear about your background, of course, but they should already know a lot before calling you or emailing you, assuming your LinkedIn profile is up to date. If you get on the phone and immediately get a question about your skills or - even worse -- your current salary, you have permission to slam the phone down! (Doesn't work with cell phones. On a cell phone, just hang up and go get a nice gelato.)

Good recruiters respect your boundaries

A recruiter-candidate relationship is based on trust, and that is something a recruiter has to earn. Anyone who calls a stranger (you) out of the blue and asks personal questions is not someone who knows Thing One about trust. Run away and find a better recruiter or reach out to hiring managers on your own.

Don't let a recruiter tell you that you MUST do anything as a candidate. It is not true. Every decision in your job search is up to you.

You do not have to call in sick to go to a job interview. You can tell the recruiter you are not available for interviews during working hours because you are employed (if you are in stealth job search mode).

You don't have to work for free during the hiring process. You can set boundaries with any recruiter you choose to work with – and you must!

Good recruiters keep their candidates posted

I have sat on panels with bad recruiters and heard them say to the audience "If I represent you, I won't call you unless there's something to report." In plain English that means "Who cares about you?"

If the recruiter isn't willing to send you an email message once a week whether there's news from a particular employer or not, leave them in the dust. If they are good at their jobs, there should be news -- it's their job to get it!

Good recruiters don't squash candidates' expectations

Bad recruiters talk down their candidates' expectations. Good recruiters are honest with you. They willt tell you, for instance, what level of salary they think your background can command in the talent market.

They won't say, "You think pretty highly of yourself, don't you?" They will respect your viewpoint, even if they disagree with you.

Good recruiters don't say "This is what the client wants, so we have to go along with it"

Maybe the recruiter has to go along with an employer's goofy requirements, but that is their problem and has nothing to do with you.

As soon as a recruiter tells you "We have to go along with the client's requirements" you know that your resume is in the wrong hands.

Get out of that relationship and stop letting somebody else tell you what you have to do -- particularly somebody who makes money when you accept an offer!

That's unethical and it's not in your best interests. Run!

Good recruiters shepherd job candidates through the process

Our client Nathan was working with a few recruiters on his job search. One of them called to tell Nathan that he was being invited to an interview at the company's headquarters in Alabama. The recruiter spent twenty minutes talking Nathan through the process - how they'd book the flights, what would happen on Nathan's interviewing trip and so on, leaving out no detail. That man is a terrific recruiter.

Another recruiter called Nathan a few days later to tell him that one of his prospective employers needed him to take a drug screen.

It wasn't going to work -- the employer needed the drug screen to be taken within 48 hours, but Nathan was in Alabama.

Nathan sent an email message to the recruiter, saying 'I'm out of town. I can take the drug screen when I get back on Friday.'

The recruiter didn't spend ten seconds with Nathan on the phone working out the drug-screen issue.

"Catch an earlier flight home," she said in a voicemail message. "Pay the hundred-dollar change fee. It's worth it."

It wasn't worth it to Nathan.

He liked the Alabama people a lot better than the hurry-up-and-drug-test people, and what sealed the deal was the professionalism of the Alabama recruiter versus the toadishness of the drug-screen recruiter.

Case closed! Nathan loves his new job. He trusted his gut, and you can do the same thing.

Good recruiters are honest

Sometimes a recruiter will tell you "I know you really believe you're qualified for this job, but this is not the right job for you."

Don't hate the recruiter for telling you what they believe. Bad recruiters shine you on.

They tell you for weeks "I'm waiting to hear back from the client" as though they have no phone and no email to reach out to the client and say "Hey, what about my candidate?"

Recruiters who don't speak up and insist that their clients behave as professionally as they expect you to do are people you don't need in your life.

Good recruiters focus on long-term relationships

Good recruiters don't treat you as a throwaway commodity. If you don't get one job they pitch you for, they'll keep in touch and let you know about other jobs at their client organizations.

I have recruiter friends who have worked with the same candidates for twenty-five years. They are great recruiters. Lousy recruiters only call you when they believe they can make a quick buck by selling you to an employer. If you don't feel good about the relationship, believe me -- you don't want the job.

Good recruiters give feedback

After a job interview, everyone wants feedback! Good recruiters use the same thoughtful listening skills that made you trust them to get feedback for you after every single job interview.

If you don't get feedback beyond "Next!" after a job interview, something is broken. If the recruiter tells you "The employer won't return my calls," what does that signal? Your recruiter has no juice with the employer. That's not a good sign.

Good recruiters focus on trust rather than fear

Bad recruiters start every candidate relationship with fear. They try to get you off guard. They ask personal questions that are none of their business. Good recruiters would never dream of doing that. They cultivate long-term relationships with candidates like you - mutually beneficial relationships that morph easily into friendship.

Wait for a recruiter who respects you. You may have to slam a lot of doors on the way to meeting the right recruiter(s) for you. It's worth the wait!

ARE YOUR JOB ADS ATTRACTING TALENT – OR DRIVING TALENT AWAY?

It's easy to see what makes a great job ad.

A great job ad is one that gets people excited about working for you, and then makes it easy for them to learn more. Most job ads fail on both counts.

Most job ads start off by telling job seekers about the high opinion your company has of itself. They don't give any evidence for the opinion -- they just tell us "With a long history of excellence, XYZ Inc. is a leader in its industry."

Anyone could say that. What makes your company a great place to work? That's what inquiring minds want to know.

The worst job ads don't even speak to the people who are reading them. They speak right past their readers, using the third person like this:

The Selected Candidate will possess twenty years of search-engine optimization experience, the ability to play the trombone while riding a unicycle and excellent Greek skills (ancient Greek) plus a current taxi driver's license.

When you talk past the job seeker in the third person, referring to The Selected Candidate instead of "you" the way any other kind of ad would do, you're saying "We don't know who The Selected Candidate will be, but we can say for sure it won't be **you!**"

Any candidate with an ounce of self-esteem is going to zip right past your job ad and go to work for somebody else -- and can we blame them?

The best job ads tell you why the job will be fun and interesting.

It's easy to write a job ad with a human voice in it. Here's an example:

My grandfather started Acme Explosives in 1955 to get coyotes the stick dynamite they need for their projects, and now Acme is going strong with manufacturing on three continents.

We've just received approval to ship modular, assemble-on-site stick dynamite products through UPS and trucking firms and we're launching our first e-commerce site.

We need an E-Commerce Operations Manager to run the online sales and marketing part of our business and coordinate with Production and Purchasing.

The job will be fast and furious and full of new adventures as you design our back-end operations to support our e-commerce business. You'll work closely with our inside and outside sales folks, Marketing and everyone else on our team.

Who will love this job? It might you if you like creating new processes, love to juggle projects and know something about e-commerce and online merchandising.

If you think this $70-$75K assignment might be right for you, please write to me at chuck@acmegoboom.com and tell me *why in 300 words. Include your <u>LinkedIn</u> profile URL in your message and skip the resume.*

One of us will get back to you within 48 hours of receiving your message or the next business day.

Thanks for checking out Acme Explosives and wishing you a dynamite day!

Chuck Jones is the CEO of Acme Explosives.

He's ready to read 300-word messages for a week or two to find the right person for his needs. He's ready to reply to everyone who responds.

It's a new day in the talent marketplace. We can talk about talent forever but the organizations that act on their beliefs about the importance of talent to their success will win not only the "talent wars" but blow past their business goals as well.

THE RIGHT WAY TO POST JOB OPENINGS

The right way to post job openings is to start small.

Make your job opportunity known to a specific group of people who are more likely than not to be qualified for and interested in the role or know people who are.

The best place to start is with your own employees, customers and vendors, social media followers and friends of the company. These are people who already know your organization and, we hope, are cheering you on.

Pay a bonus to anyone -- yep, I said anyone -- who sends you the candidate you eventually hire. Now you've got a double win -- you're promoting your job ads to people who already know and love you, and you're paying them to deliver the right hire to your door. Make it easy to forward resumes and make email introductions.

If you're still directing candidates into an automated, Black Hole recruiting pit, you are going to miss out on people who could help your organization compete. Who can afford to do that?

THE HORRIBLE TRUTH ABOUT 'PASSIVE' JOB CANDIDATES

"Passive" job candidates are living their lives, not thinking about job-hunting, when an employer swoops in to contact them about potential job opportunities.

"Passive" job candidates are popular with employers these days. They want to find their own candidates rather than running job ads and talking with the job seekers who respond to those ads.

These days, employer representative and in-house recruiters reach out to currently employed working people to share job opportunities nearly as often as third-party recruiters do.

Employers call these working people "passive" job candidates because they are not job-hunting when the conversation starts.

A "passive job seeker" is anything but passive. They get up and go to work and take care of a million details every day the same way we all do. They are only passive from the employer's point of view.

When I was a corporate HR person, I beat the bushes for qualified candidates. I went to trade shows and handed out my business card. I talked to friends of our employees and friends of their friends. I was out in the community all the time. That is how we have to recruit if we want to get great people.

We can't be passive ourselves!

There will always be people who are thinking about changing jobs and would welcome an overture from an organization like yours.

Yet I am skeptical about the "passive candidate" attraction craze because it reinforces the idea that a candidate we "find" on LinkedIn and reach out to is inherently more desirable and appealing to us than candidates who reach out to us.

That's a terrible outlook.

We can agree that any company that spends much of its recruiting energy working to engage passive candidates must also make it clear that their own employees are welcome and encouraged to job-hunt while working, because the firm is enticing people who work elsewhere to do just that.

Secondly, we must assume that companies who work to engage passive candidates will never lay off any of their own employees. Who could be crass enough to lay off employees while clinging to the belief that only currently employed candidates are worth considering for employment?

No one who follows business news at any level of depth could be unaware that hundreds of thousands or millions of fantastic and capable people have gotten laid off from their jobs through no fault of their own. They are not second-tier job candidates.

If anything, they are closer to the talent marketplace and more in touch with their abilities and the needs of employers than folks who haven't job-hunted or changed jobs in years.

To stratify the so-called "talent community" into two levels where currently employed candidates outrank unemployed folks is the opposite of leadership.

I wish the people who moon over passive-candidate engagement would keep in mind that there is nothing magical about hiring an employed person vs. an unemployed person.

You have your third-party recruiting partners to maintain their longitudinal relationships with candidates and make introductions for you to brilliant people you don't know already.

Fixating on pulling passive candidates out of their current roles and into your shop is not going to solve whatever is wrong with your culture and your recruiting system and mindset, but an honest organizational self-appraisal will.

TEN REASONS TO HIRE SOMEONE WITHOUT A COLLEGE DEGREE

Dear Liz,

There is a debate in my company over the importance of a four-year college degree for our entry-level staff professional jobs.

The company currently requires a four-year degree for our new hires in every exempt job and many non-exempt roles, too. Some of our managers, including me, are questioning the wisdom of that hiring requirement.

In previous roles, I have hired numerous candidates who lacked a four-year degree and I've never had a problem teaching them how to do their jobs.

I think my company is behind the times. I think our hiring process would be easier and faster if we expanded the pool of qualified candidates to include qualified candidates who lack a four-year degree.

That could be someone with equivalent work experience or a two-year degree with additional training, or any number of other career and educational histories.

What is your take? Do you feel that a four-year degree is an iron-clad prerequisite for a staff level professional role?

Thanks Liz -

Yours,
Naomi

Dear Naomi,

A four-year degree requirement for new hires is seldom really about the job requirements.

Many organizations require a four-year degree primarily because it makes their recruiting process easier.

Any hard-and-fast hiring criterion is a waste of talent, money and other resources, but most companies build their recruiting processes to be mechanical and uniform — not human, smart or cost-effective.

In my experience any bright and curious person can learn to perform almost any business role. How else would so many self-made entrepreneurs without degrees have become as successful as they are?

They figure out how to do their jobs. That's what everybody has to do — college degree or no.

Here are ten good reasons to hire someone without a four-year degree into a staff professional job:

1. Some people learn best in school, and other people don't. They learn by doing. You will miss out on a huge talent population if you screen out brilliant, capable and hard-working people for whom the classroom is not a good learning environment — but for whom your plant or office would be.

2. Some people worked through the years other folks were in college. They learned on the job. In contrast, some new graduates from four-year institutions have never worked at all. They have never held a job. Which candidate is going to make a bigger contribution to your organization, sooner?

3. Some folks could not afford college when they were of traditional college age. They might do brilliantly in college later in their lives, but right now they don't have any

formal education past high school. Unless your company requires a new hire's four-year degree to map perfectly to their job function, why would you care very much whether your sharp new employee has spent the past four years in school — or working, and learning as they go?

4. Some hiring managers believe that a four-year degree is the mark of a mature adult versus a rowdy kid. That is not a good assumption. Some kids are studious, and some are not. Many kids make it through a four-year degree program without maturing in any way. It's all about the kid — not their degree or lack thereof.

5. Community college instructors are real-world practitioners who can teach their students not only their subject but also the mechanics of their trade and how to make a career in it. They teach those things alongside the "how tos" of the profession. They teach from real-world examples. However, many community colleges don't offer four-year degrees. Why penalize a student for training under a working professional versus a university professor? If anything, we would expect businesses to prefer the former to the latter.

6. Some folks graduate from high school and join the military, or volunteer to serve their communities. It is likely to take longer for these students to earn a degree because of their military service or volunteering commitment. Their service is critical and beneficial to a healthy society, so why make it harder for military veterans and former volunteers to get hired into responsible positions the minute their service commitment is complete?

7. When you open your hiring pipeline to people with more varied backgrounds you will increase the diversity of your new hires — bringing in new points of view, new ideas and talent from a wider spectrum than you will ever get hiring strictly graduates of four-year degree programs.

8. When you hire a mix of four-year college graduates and people without college degrees, everybody will learn something new. Your department managers may learn the most!

9. When you drop the iron-clad four-year-degree requirement from your hiring protocol, you will become the employer of choice in your area for smart, accomplished folks without college degrees — people who can help your business tomorrow.

10. Whenever you re-evaluate and question your standard ways of doing things, you grow as a person and a professional, and your fellow leaders grow as well.

Hiring only college grads is lazy, and we all know it.

Spending four years on campus doesn't make you smarter. It doesn't make you more creative. It teaches you certain things that may or may not be applicable in your new job.

It's a hiring manager's task to figure out which candidates — degree-holding or not — will make the best new hires.

All the best,
Liz

HOW BIG A SALARY CUT MUST I TAKE FOR CHANGING INDUSTRIES?

Dear Liz,

I am an inch away from a job offer with a good company but in an industry where I haven't worked before.

My feeling is that they're going to offer me the job at a pretty big drop in salary from what they were talking about paying the person they selected, with the excuse that it's a new industry for me. I want to be in a position to counter that argument if I get the offer as I expect to.

How do I explain away my zero experience in the industry to negotiate a better salary? I have a lot of experience in my old industry, and other qualifications.

Thanks,
Geri

Dear Geri,

Hurrah! I am so happy for you.

Here's the thing: they're going to hire the best person they can find for the job, right? Why would they hire someone they didn't believe was qualified?

You can open up the salary conversation with some discussion about why they want to hire you over a candidate with industry experience.

BOSS: So, Geri, we're very excited to offer you the Procurement job.

YOU: That's outstanding. I'm very eager to get started. Thanks so much, Ron. Can you please fill me in on the details?

RON: Sure, the title is Senior Procurement Manager and the salary is $64,000 to start, with three weeks' vacation and our other benefits.

YOU: Thanks, Ron. I'm so pleased that you see me as the right person for the role.

RON: Yes, indeed. So, you're accepting?

YOU: I'm happy to be having this conversation, that's for sure. The job sounds like a great fit and a really fun challenge. We're a little way apart on salary. Is this a good time to talk about that?

RON: Well — you know, you've got so many skills and we are all very impressed with you, but you don't have any experience at all in our industry. I couldn't justify the $70K base we talked about when I told the committee you've been in banking for almost all of your career.

YOU: Thanks for letting me know, Ron. I can see the difficulty. The thing is, I would be wary of taking a job where there was a concern that I was less than fully qualified for the job.

RON: I didn't say that. We all thought you should get the job.

YOU: I appreciate that, Ron. Did you say everyone in the selection group thought I was the best candidate?

RON: Yes, we did, except you don't have any experience in our industry.

YOU: So I'm thinking that you had other candidates who did have industry experience - you must have had, right?

RON: We did, but we all wanted you in the job.

YOU: Thanks! You know Ron, I am confused. If industry experience were critical to the role, I'm sure you would have hired a candidate who has industry experience. If it is not essential to

have industry experience in this job and you feel I can do the
job, why not pay me what the job pays?

RON: Er — yeah. I'll talk to Boris, our CFO, tomorrow and get
back to you.

I'm not saying it will play out exactly this way, Ger, but you see
the idea.

If you are the right person for the job, then you're the right
person to get paid whatever they would have paid whomever they
decided to hire.

It makes no sense to say that you beat out the other candidates
(people with industry experience) for the role but still deserve to
be paid less than one of the industry-experienced candidates would
have been paid.

When in doubt about whether to negotiate a job offer, do it.
Remember that only the people who get you, deserve you.

Cheers,
Liz

THE HORRIBLE TRUTH ABOUT
ONE-WAY VIDEO INTERVIEWS

Dear Liz,

I was asked to take a one-way video interview last week.

It took me some time to understand what the HR lady wanted because I couldn't believe they would ask me to answer questions in front of my computer with no live person on the other end of the line. I think it's awful.

I declined to take the interview. I don't want to work for a company that would stick me in front of a piece of software and ask me to talk into my microphone.

If they don't have time to talk with me live, they can hire somebody else.

What is your take on one-way video interviews?

Thanks,

Dear Richard,

If companies screen people out using one-way video interviews, they don't have to meet as many people face to face.

There is an equation implied in the one-way video interview paradigm. The equation says that the interviewer's wish to not be bothered meeting people like you is greater than your wish to talk to a live person when you are interested in a job.

Dehumanizing recruiting practices like one-way video interviews will stay in use as long as job seekers submit to them.

Sadly, one-way video interviewing is not the only dehumanizing interviewing practice, but it is becoming more common. If all a company wants is a printout of your answers to common interview questions, why do they make you interview with your voice at all?

A fast, effective and cost-conscious recruiting process does not include one-way video interviews.

Employers who turn to this recruiting practice are missing the point of process design. They fundamentally misunderstand recruiting, which is a sales and marketing process much more than a winnowing-out process.

They need to rethink their entire recruiting strategy and mindset.

They are making their job more complicated than it needs to be, costing their companies money and worst of all, alienating the talent community in the worst possible way.

You know there are employers who will respect you enough to interact with you when they want to know you. Your job is to keep up the search until you find people who resonate at your frequency, as the one-way-video-interview folks so clearly do not.

Yours,
Liz

WHY I WON'T HIRE ANYONE WHO'S SMARTER THAN I AM

Dear Liz,

I read your columns and recommend them. I like how you bring real-world knowledge into the conversation every time.

My Director loves to say, "Whenever you hire someone, hire someone smarter than you are!" but I'm not going to do that.

The working world is too volatile. If I hire someone who can do my job, there's no reason for my company to keep me.

They can promote the person I hired (who's smarter than me) and get rid of me and my expensive salary. What manager would put themselves at risk that way?

My Director hires people who are capable (like me) but clearly a step down from him in experience and knowledge. I don't know anybody who hires differently. Why would I hire someone who's qualified for my job?

Thanks Liz --
Josef

Dear Josef,

When we say, "Hire someone who's smarter than you are!" it doesn't necessarily mean you should hire someone who could step into your job tomorrow.

As you point out, if you hire people who are massively overequipped for the jobs they're given, you are lucky to end up with a bunch of frustrated employees.

"Smart" doesn't mean "overqualified." It means that someone has a brain and isn't afraid to use it. Smart people ask a lot of questions. They are intellectually curious.

Being smart, of course, is not the same as being highly educated. Everyone knows at least one highly educated person who is not nearly as smart as they think they are.

Likewise, we all know people who have little to no formal education and are brilliant people -- they don't need formal education for their brilliance to come out!

You have a fear that is very common and very normal -- the fear that if you hire talented people onto your team, one of them might threaten your role or even replace you.

That can happen, but only in a toxic organization where people are dishonest with one another. Assuming that you trust your Director, you can hire smart people with confidence.

Why would anyone hire someone who is smarter than the manager him- or herself is?

Hiring great people makes your department and your company more successful and makes your job easier. Brilliant employees make you look like the confident, talent-aware manager you are.

Hiring smart people builds bench strength in your organization that will make it easier for you to step up to a bigger job, knowing that one or two people are standing by ready to step into your role. That's where your confidence comes in!

If the only scenario you can imagine is one where your smart underling pushes you out of your job, then you have a leak in your fuel tank!

When you can envision a future where your brilliant team member takes your position and you walk into a bigger, more exciting one -- then you will see the benefits of hiring the very best employees you can find!

All the best,
Liz

THE 10 WORST REASONS TO REJECT A JOB APPLICANT

Dear Liz,

I am job hunting. I've had three first interviews and two second interviews so far.

One of the first interviews was a bust. I knew as soon as I got there it was going to be weird. I did the interview sitting in a tiny, dark, smelly conference room with the most obnoxious interviewer ever.

The company itself was super sketchy. There were about 30 or 40 people working in ugly, old, beige cubicles and not talking. The whole place was silent. It was dirty, too. The manager "Bob" interviewed me. He was so rude you wouldn't believe it.

The minute Bob and I sat down in the interview room he started quizzing me about my background, asking me detailed questions about every job I've ever held.

I felt like a criminal suspect.

Bob interviewed me like a police interrogator. He acted like he didn't believe anything on my resume.

I gave him my entire career story in excruciating detail. He was practically sneering. I wanted to ask him, "If my background is so unimpressive, why did you invite me here?"

We finally got to the job I held in 2004. I barely remember that job. I answered Bob's questions about my 2004 job as well as I could.

Then he asked me, "Why is there a six-month gap after the job you left in 2004?"

I said, "I worked for a company briefly in that six-month period, but it really wasn't relevant to the work I do now, so I left it off my resume."

Bob said, "Well, I thank you for your honesty, but that omission is disqualifying. This interview is over."

I almost laughed out loud. Poor Bob thinks that getting a job with his ratty beige cubicle company is the be-all and end-all. I said, "That's fine. I can show myself out," and I left.

Is that the most ridiculous thing you've ever heard? A six-month, many-years-old gap in my resume is "disqualifying."

I'm glad to know what Bob is like because he would have been my boss if I took that job. I am glad I got "disqualified" but who does Bob think he is?

What do you think, Liz?

Yours,
Angel

Dear Angel,

The penalty for being Bob is that you have to get up every morning being Bob. It must feel terrible.

Poor Bob has to make other people feel bad to make himself feel important. He is a sad human being.

Be glad you are not him!

Folks like Bob treat interviews as opportunities to throw their weight around. You figured that out right away. It is crazy to reject a qualified job candidate out of hand because they left a six-month, long-ago job off their resume.

You know all you need to know about Bob!

You can focus your job search energies on managers who aren't going to freak out about a missing job on your resume from so many years ago.

You have two good job opportunities to focus on. Forget about Bob -- and invest your energy in people who deserve your talents!

There are good reasons to say "Thanks but no thanks" to a job candidate but Bob's lame reason is not one of them.

A resume is a marketing document, not a legal document. It's up to each job seeker to include what they want to include on their resume and leave out what they want to leave out.

Here are ten ridiculous reasons to decline a job candidate:

1. Because they don't have the college degree you were hoping for, or the GPA you wanted them to have. If someone's experience suggests that they can do the job, don't be fussy about the exact degree!

   A super-high GPA means that you care very much about grades. It doesn't mean that you are smarter, more talented or more likely to succeed in the world than other people. Managers who hire based on GPA are not managers you want to work for -- even if you had a sky-high GPA.

2. Because they haven't stayed as long as you would like at some of their past jobs. People don't always choose to leave their jobs. You can't hold a short-tenure job against a job candidate when nearly everybody has been laid off at some point.

3. Because they don't have the exact job title you wanted your Selected Candidate to have. Smart recruiters know how to read between the lines! Your job ad might say that you need someone with seven years in Marketing. People can pick up marketing experience without working in the Marketing department.

You might have zero years of experience in a role with Marketing in the title, but you still might have amazing marketing experience.

4. Because they have a gap in their resume. Smart, brave people take chances. They change jobs more often than others and they take career risks. Sometimes the risks pan out and sometimes they don't. So what? It's all learning. People have personal obligations that might cause them to take a year or two away from the paid workforce. That doesn't make them less talented or valuable!

    Any company that rejects job seekers just because they have gaps on their resume doesn't deserve your talent.

5. Because they have changed industries and/or functions several times. When there was a study corporate ladder to climb, it made sense to stay in one career path. Nowadays the corporate ladder is sawdust under our feet.

    You don't get ahead by doing your job patiently and waiting for your manager to get promoted so you can move up. You would get old and die waiting for that to happen! Your best path might not be a straight path. So what?

6. Because they have held a mix of payroll and non-payroll jobs. People move in and out of organizations more easily these days. They take contract positions and they work for themselves. Smart employers do not reject candidates just because they have worked independently or on a contract basis.

7. Because they don't "look the part." The most amazing employee you will ever hire may be older or younger than you expected them to be. They may have a wildly different background than you thought they would have. They may be the exact opposite of the "perfect candidate" you envisioned. Your ability to rise out of your imagination

and snag the talented person here in the real world is what will make you a successful manager.

8. Because they won't follow your company's outdated recruiting process. If your company makes candidates fill out an online application form and somebody writes to you directly with a powerful letter, talk to them! You need initiative on your team more than you need people with a follow-the-herd mentality. They can always complete the application later, once a mutual interest is established.

9. Because they don't have every qualification listed in your job ad. Most living people don't have all the qualifications listed in any job ad. Most job ads are ridiculous -- fanciful bordering on delusional, if we are honest. As long as your candidate has the major qualifications for the job, understands what you're up against and has great ideas for your team, hire them!

10. Because it seems too risky to hire a person without the perfect background, blue-chip educational credentials and anything else your boss will expect to see in a new hire. You are the manager. Hire the right person, and let your boss learn how a non-cookie-cutter candidate can exceed their expectations!

You dodged a bullet when you "missed out" on that job opportunity. It's onward and upward from here!

Yours,
Liz

JOB SEEKERS, JUST SAY NO TO THESE 10 EMPLOYER DEMANDS

You are going to get hit with unreasonable demands from employers — or recruiters who work on behalf of employers — and you have to be ready for them.

If you aren't prepared to handle these unreasonable demands, you're likely to say "Yes!" and agree to something you shouldn't.

That's a problem for three reasons:

1. When you say "Yes, I'll gladly oblige your unreasonable request" you train the organization to mistreat you further. They won't stop until you say "Enough!"

2. When you give up your power during the hiring process, you also give up your negotiating leverage if they make you a job offer.

3. When you put up with mistreatment at the hands of employers and/or recruiters, you tell yourself "I'm not worthy of respect. I don't get to have boundaries." You'll reduce your own value and marketability by reinforcing that negative message!

The key to handling unreasonable requests from employers and recruiters is to practice saying "Here's what I can do, instead of what you've proposed" until the words roll easily off your tongue.

You'll be amazed at how much easier it is to set boundaries when you've practiced your script in advance.

If you're prepared to handle unreasonable requests, you won't stumble over your words. You'll be happy and confident, and your confidence will radiate from you.

You will educate recruiters, HR folks and hiring managers about appropriate boundaries by setting boundaries with them yourself!

If they get mad when you won't oblige their outrageous requests, that's fine. You wouldn't want to work for them anyway in that case.

Some of them will get mad, and some won't. Some of them will be embarrassed when they realize they've overstepped their bounds.

The people who deserve you will respect you for speaking up. Smart managers will realize that if you'll speak up during the interview process, then you'll also speak up on the company's behalf once you have the job.

Here are ten unreasonable demands employers make of job seekers:

1. They will ask you for your past and/or current salary details. No dice! That's none of their business.

2. They will ask you for your references before you've even met them.

3. They will drag you through endless interviews without telling you how much the job pays. Don't go along with that -- ask them "What is the salary range for this job?"

4. They will ask you to perform work for free — creating a marketing plan, for instance, or writing a proposal — during the interview process.

5. They will ask you to come back for interview after interview. Three interviews are plenty, apart from very specific special circumstances.

6. They will grill you for free consulting advice during your interviews.

7. They will leave you in silence for weeks and then call or email you one day and say, "Your next interview is tomorrow." Forget that!

8. They will tell you to bring in written proof of your last salary.

9. They will tell you "We love you, but we want to meet other candidates," and then expect you to wait around while they re-run the job ad and screen resumes all over again. They are looking for someone as awesome as you are — but cheaper!

10. They will tell you that they want to hire you, but at a lower starting salary than what you and they already agreed on.

Here's how to handle each of these scenarios.

Past Salary Request

Recruiter: So, what were you earning at your last job?
You: In this job search I'm focusing on jobs in the $55,000 range. Is this job in that range?

Hand Over Your References

Recruiter: So, why don't you send me your list of references now, so I'll have it in case this client wants to interview you.
You: I will be happy to give you or the employer my references after I've met them and there's a mutual interest in continuing the conversation. Right now, I can send you my resume.

Multiple Interviews with No Salary Range Information

Recruiter: Good news! They want you to come back for a second interview next Thursday.

You: Great! Let me check my schedule. Let's make sure we are in sync regarding salary. My salary target is $55,000. Will that salary work for the client?

Work for Free

Recruiter: They liked you a lot at your first interview. The next step is for you to create a spreadsheet listing their ten competitors' websites with your reviews of the usability, content and design on each one.

You: I'm happy to donate an hour of work to show that I understand the role. I can sign up for a one-hour project. It won't be an in-depth review of ten websites, but a quick overview. Will that work for your client?

More Than Three Interviews

Recruiter: I thought they were ready to make a decision, but it turns out that they want to see you again, next Friday.

You: I understand it can be hard to make a hiring decision but if I come back for a fourth interview, I have to receive a verbal offer before I leave — or the news that they've decided to hire someone else. Can they agree to that?

Recruiter: I doubt it. They're going to need time to make a decision.

You: I totally understand, and in that case, they should probably hire another candidate.

Recruiter: Let me see what I can do.

Free Consulting

Hiring Manager: How would you solve our marketing problems?

You: First I would define the problem and clarify your goals. There may be many stakeholders with different ideas of what the end goal is. Then I'd start my research - collecting data, interviewing your team members and your customers, and putting an array of options together. I'd sit down with you and go through the options and their costs, and we'd make a decision.

Manager: But I mean -- what's the right answer?

You: That's what we will determine! It would be irresponsible of me to venture a guess as to what you should do right now, sitting here. You are smart and so are your teammates and you haven't settled on the right answer yet. I wouldn't presume to say what the right answer is, until I have the facts!

Weeks of Silence, Then "Jump!"

Recruiter: Good news! I know it's been six weeks since we heard from my client, but they want you to come back and interview again tomorrow.

You: I wrote that company off three weeks ago. If they want to hire me, they should make an offer. Or I can consult with them for a fee. I have no reason to think they're serious about hiring me. They might be kicking tires. The manager Sarah can call me if she wants, and we can talk about it.

Recruiter: Okay, great.

Written Proof of Your Last Salary

Recruiter: They all like you! Now they need your last year's W-2 to prove your earnings.

You: I can understand why they want that data, just like I would love to know what their executives get paid — but I understand that information is confidential. My salary history is confidential, too. If they think I'm worth the $85,000 I'm asking for, they should hire me at that salary. If not, I understand, and we can part ways.

Wait While We Interview More People

Hiring Manager: We all think you're amazing — we just want to see more candidates. It shouldn't take too long. We're re-running the job ad now.

You: I understand. If you aren't quite sure I am the person you need, I will drop out of the process. I'm sure you understand that I can only take a job if I have a full vote of confidence. If you want to make me an offer, let's do it this week. Otherwise I'll move on to other opportunities.

Hiring Manager: Okay. That's fair. I'll talk to my colleagues and let you know our decision today.

We're Starting You Off at A Lower Salary

Hiring Manager: We want to make you an offer! You and I talked about $75,000 but since you're new to the industry, we're going to start you at $67,500 and gradually move you up.

You: Thanks for that information! I am new to the industry — that's true. Did you interview people with experience in your industry?

Hiring Manager: Well — yes.

You: You interviewed people with industry experience, but you still decided to hire me?

Hiring Manager: That's right.

You: If you decided to hire me over people with industry experience, then you should pay me what the job pays. I can only take the job at the salary we discussed — I'm sure you understand.

Hiring Manager: Your argument makes sense! You are a good negotiator.

You: That will come in handy when I'm negotiating with your suppliers!

IN RECRUITING, THE CUSTOMER IS NOT ALWAYS RIGHT

We all have customers, whether they are external to our companies or sitting at the next desk. Every job produces output that other people rely on.

When you are working as an internal recruiter or as a third-party recruiter who finds new talent for your clients, you have customers.

Since I write about recruiting all the time, I hear this sentiment from recruiters all the time, too:

> *I agree with what you say about how to treat job candidates, Liz, but my clients don't. They want me to do things the traditional way – getting a candidate's current and past salary information right up front, for instance. I'm a vendor to my client, so I can't tell them I won't do what they want. I have to do what they tell me to do, or they'll hire someone else to recruit for them!*

We can empathize with a recruiter who's caught in a bind between following their conscience and values to treat job candidates like gold, and a client's desire to handle candidates with much less finesse.

It's easy for the client to say, "This is what I want -- give it to me, or else!" because they are not the person who's going to be speaking with candidates, at least not right away. Clients, by virtue of having you recruiting for them rather than doing their own recruiting, are removed from the marketplace.

They may not know that it has been good recruiting practice to ask a candidate for their salary target, rather than salary history, for several years now even in places where it's legal to ask for salary history.

Your clients may not know that it is impolite and bad recruiting practice to call a candidate and start interviewing them before sharing information about the job with them.

Every recruiter will face an unreasonable client (or more than one) over their career. The recruiters who understand what they bring to their clients, internal or external, will teach and guide their clients rather than racing off to do their clients' bidding down to the smallest detail.

Do you run the risk that when you set boundaries with your clients, establish expectations for them (how to treat your candidates, for instance, or even how to treat you) they may end the relationship?

Yes, you do.

Whether we work for ourselves or for a larger firm, we are forced to make practical and ethical decisions every day. We learn over time that the only way to grow our muscles is to use them.

You may upset an internal or external client by telling them more truth than are ready for, but that is their problem and not yours. Your job is not to protect people from reality but to help them understand the real world of talent acquisition in which you, they and your candidates operate.

It's a new day. We are learning to reinvent recruiting and leadership practices for humans. Recruiters are in a better position than most to teach and guide their clients how to recruit amazing people by making the candidate experience central to every recruiting activity and conversation.

TEN SIMPLE WAYS TO HIRE GREAT PEOPLE, FAST

HR is not the easiest job in the world.

It's hard to advise a cranky CEO or get an opinionated management team to work together.

It's not that easy to make everybody on your team feel heard and valued.

However, recruiting should not be as hard as it is.

We need to stop blaming external forces and start looking critically at our own recruiting practices if we want to recruit more effectively.

The educational system is not responsible for training students to your specifications. Society is not responsible for delivering purple unicorns to your front door, scrubbed and ready to "hit the ground running."

I love recruiting because it requires strategy and a human touch. It is more fun to seek out amazing people and sell them on your opportunities than to arrange a cattle call and screen most of the applicants out.

Inviting people into your recruiting pipeline just to send most of them away is a terrible message for your company to send to your community!

Sadly, too many recruiters and HR people see their jobs as vetting jobs rather than sales and marketing assignments.

It is easy to hire great people.

You have to pay them fairly -- that's the first step. If you are a recruiter or an HR person charged with hiring new employees and you know your company's or client's salary ranges are too low, you can't take on the assignment.

You have to push back. It's not only their brand that's at stake -- your brand and your integrity are at stake, too!

If the client won't budge, drop them and get a new client. Mother Nature is the best teacher, but her lessons are not always fun. That's okay! Our muscles get huge every time we step into fear and come out stronger on the other side.

If you work for a company that won't pay people appropriately for their roles, keep sounding the alarm but launch a stealth job at the same time and go someplace where talent -- including your talent -- is valued.

Recruiting is easy when you do it well. Here are ten steps to get you started:

1. Instead of writing job descriptions full of tasks and duties, think about and talk about -- and only then begin to write about -- the major problem each new role relieves. What terrible things would befall your company if this new employee were not on the job? Nobody wants to come in and take over a list of boring tasks and duties. When you write a job ad, you must tell candidates (and anybody who could refer candidates to you) what kinds of dragons you want them to slay!

2. Write a job ad that sells the job rather than listing all the picky qualifications you think your new hire has to bring with them. The truth is that most of those qualifications are not really necessary -- they only salve the hiring manager's ego or match a dusty spec sitting on hard drive in HR, unconnected to the actual needs of your business.

3. Instead of sending interested applicants to the gaping maw of an applicant tracking system, invite them to send you a Pain Letter™ with a link to their LinkedIn profile, instead.

4. Get back to the applicants in the order their replies are received and do it fast -- within 48 hours. Tell them you received their materials, and tell them in a human voice, with a human email signature at the bottom of the message! You cannot attract great people through mechanical means or by using robots to communicate with them.

5. When you begin to schedule interviews, tell each applicant to prepare questions for your interviewers. If your HR screeners or internal recruiters won't be able to answer a thoughtful applicants' questions about the job, team up your recruiters with hiring managers for joint interviews. That way your recruiters will learn how to answer relevant questions candidates are likely to ask.

6. When each job interview begins, let the candidate go first. Let them ask questions for you to answer. If the entire interview is a Q & A session in which the candidate asks questions and your interviewers answer them, that's fine. You will learn much more about a job candidate from the questions they think up than you will from their answers to your scripted interview questions.

7. Talk about salary on the first interview to save everybody's time.

8. Show finalist candidates the employee handbook, details on any bonus plans that will apply to them, the work area, and anything else they want to see. Let them meet the team members and vice versa. Return their email and voice mail messages fast. They are your company's future!

9. When you don't hire someone, invite them to join your company's talent community on whatever platform you

like. Keep these friends of your company in the loop with company news and new job openings. Get creative! Make these folks eligible for referral bonuses just as your current (and former?) employees are.

10. Finally, keep the human voice and human element in your recruiting process from start to finish. Get rid of any harsh, bureaucratic language you might use to communicate with candidates now. Remember that there is only one fuel source to power your company's success, and that fuel source is the positive energy on your team.

HR folks and recruiters have a huge impact on the success of your company when they are tuned in to the power of trust. Now is a great time to assess your recruiting process and see whether it is doing its job for you. Now is a great time to improve it!

PUT THE SALARY RANGE IN YOUR JOB AD, ALREADY

Why don't employers put their salary ranges into their job ads? We know why: they want to see whether they can hire someone at the rock bottom price.

They may have $65-$80K budgeted, but if someone walks in who can do the job at $58K, they are likely to be hired at that very salary level.

Why else would employers keep their salary ranges secret? I cannot think of a good reason, and I've been an HR person for over thirty years.

It is unethical and tacky to ask candidates for their current salary level even where it is still legal to do so, but internal and external recruiters around the world do it every day. When they are honest, they say "Why pay more than we have to?"

When you ask a candidate for their current salary or salary history, you're saying "We value you based on what another organization paid you. That's the only way we know how to value your talents."

That is the same as saying "I have no business being a recruiter, or a manager. I'm clueless."

As businesspeople we make judgment calls every day. If I meet you and spend an hour with you, I will be able to tell you at the end of that hour what I think you can command dollars-and-cents-wise in the talent market where you live.

I don't need to know your past or current salaries to make that determination.

Any competent HR leader could do the same thing. Any competent recruiter could do it, too. When someone asks you "What did they pay you at your last job?" you know that the question has everything to do with keeping as much information behind the veil as possible. That gives an employer a negotiating advantage.

The sensible and ethical thing to do is to include a salary range in every job ad. That way, people who don't want the job at the salary you're willing to pay won't waste their time and your time applying for the position.

If every employer or a lot of them start posting their salary ranges, employers would save a lot of time and money.

Candidates would save time and aggravation. Anybody who took the time to read job ads as a market research practice would soon learn what various jobs pay at various organizations. As an employer, wouldn't it be helpful for the local talent community to understand your pay levels?

If you ask a recruiter, "What's the salary range for this job?" you should get a definite answer.

If you expect a candidate to begin a conversation with you, understand that you owe them a few things in exchange for their time and attention.

One of those reasonable expectations is the salary range for any job you reach out to the candidate to discuss.

PART THREE

THE INTERVIEW

HOW TO RUIN A JOB INTERVIEW IN UNDER FIVE MINUTES

Setting: A sunny office, mid-afternoon. COCO the cat is sleeping on a pillow. LIZ is drawing at the conference table. The phone rings.

RRRRRRRRING!

LIZ (pressing the button to operate the speaker): Liz Ryan! Is this Denise?

DENISE *(on the phone)*: Yes! Hi, Liz - it's nice to meet you!

LIZ: Nice to meet you, too!

DENISE: Thanks for making time to speak with me about my story.

LIZ: No problem!

DENISE: My editor assigned me this story. It's a piece about interviewing mistakes -- how to ruin a job interview through lack of preparation, and that kind of thing.

LIZ: Great. Do you have questions for me?

DENISE: Well, what is the number one thing that causes job interviews to fall apart?

LIZ: It's what you said -- lack of preparation. Not taking the process seriously enough, and not giving it enough thought. Dialing it in, you might say.

DENISE: And with all the articles that have been written on this topic, why do you think that people still make the same interviewing mistakes?

LIZ: It's hard to blame them. Where would they go to be trained in good interviewing technique? It's not like they learn it in school.

DENISE: That's a good point. So how can people get better at interviewing?

LIZ: One way is to really think through the job opening. Think about what's important in the job -- not just the standard interview questions and standard answers.

DENISE: Does Human Workplace™ teach people how to think through the job opening and prepare for a job interview?

LIZ: For sure!

DENISE: So, how would you advise a client to begin their preparation?

LIZ: Well, you've got job ad, right? You've got a job opening and a hiring manager who went to great trouble to get that job opening approved.

Chief Financial Officers and other financial people are not in a rush to approve new job openings. There has to be big pain, or they would wait and fill the job later, or never fill it.

DENISE: So, you have to think about what that pain might be?

LIZ: Unless you work for the company, and then you can just ask the department manager.

DENISE: Wait a second -- you said, "Unless you work for the company." If someone's looking for a job, they're not already working there -- how could they ask the manager?

LIZ: What audience are you writing the story for? I thought we were talking about the interviewer.

DENISE: No, this is a story for job seekers.

LIZ: Really? Oh, that's my mistake. I figured you were writing a story for interviewers, because most of the not-prepping-for-interviews problems and the dialing-it-in problems I see are not on the job seeker side of the desk. They're on the interviewer's side.

DENISE: Okay, wait! Now I'm confused. An interviewer has to prepare for a job interview?

LIZ: Definitely! Sadly, way too many job interviewers just go through the motions -- like you mentioned, following the standard script. That's a huge disservice to their colleagues, their customers and their shareholders. It's a massive insult to the job applicant who spent a lot of time learning about the company and preparing questions. It also doesn't do a good job of helping you determine which candidates are best suited to the role.

DENISE: Why not?

LIZ: In the traditional interviewing set-up we focus all of our energy on vetting the candidate and very little if any of it on selling them on the opportunity. We assume they're sold on the opportunity, because they showed up for the interview. We focus on our needs and not theirs, and we don't even do a good job of evaluating whether a person can do the job or not.

How could we tell the best candidates from any other candidate using the awful, scripted questions every candidate hates? I'm talking about questions like, "What's your greatest weakness?" and "Where do you see yourself in five years?" How on earth would questions like this help us make better hires? They wouldn't!

DENISE: Can you give me an example?

LIZ: People have their biases and prejudices, right? We all have them. We can surmount them if we are aware of them, but most interviewers don't even stop to do that. They walk around with ideas in their heads that they believe are real and don't consciously think about, much less talk about.

They might believe that people who know their weaknesses and are willing to tell strangers about their weaknesses are better hires. Is there any evidence for that? Heck, no! Those interviewers don't care. It's their personal opinion that unless you can come up with a really good weakness on the spot and spit it out, you're not the right person for the job.

We can't even say for sure what a 'weakness' is, or why everyone must have one, but a lot of interviewers insist that not only do people have them, but it's appropriate for a job seeker to tell the interview -- a perfect stranger -- what those weaknesses are! They say, "It shows self-awareness." Self-awareness cuts both ways!

The question "What is your greatest weakness" shouldn't even be legal -- it has nothing to do with a person's qualifications for the job. But we have all grown up with the idea that the interviewer sits on a higher perch than the job seeker does, and therefore calls the shots. We see this belief acted out in job interviews every day.

DENISE: I never thought about it before, but you're right. It's almost as though the job seeker is expected to put on a show for the interviewer's pleasure.

LIZ: That's the whole story, except in those organizations and for those managers who are aware of that bias and work to neutralize it. A lot of people don't.

They firmly believe that one of the benefits of being a manager or a recruiter or HR person is that you get to run applicants through their paces. There's no business logic behind it -- it's just a process that we cast in stone a hundred years ago and haven't thought about since.

If you needed a plumber to come to your house and get your kid's sock out of the tub drain, would you dream of subjecting the plumber to your list of goofy questions? Of course not! The plumber would never stand for it.

DENISE: So, you believe that it's job interviewers, and not job applicants, who have the most to learn about interviewing?

LIZ: Even before anybody learns anything, it's the job interviewers who have the most to UN-learn. Step one: burn the interview script! It's a hundred years out of date. Get off the script and have a human conversation.

DENISE: You teach people how to do that?

LIZ: Yes, and it's easy to learn once you shift your mindset. It's much more fun to interview people in a human way than to grill them like suspects in a police interrogation room!

DENISE: Wow, this is not what I expected. I thought you were going to talk about how job seekers ruin their chances at a job by blowing job interviews.

LIZ: The idea that as a job candidate you can "blow" a job interview by answering a question less than perfectly is part of the problem. We treat a job interview as an audition for "America's Got Talent." It should be a free-flowing two-way conversation. The organization is selling itself to the candidate – or should be – at least as much as the candidate sells the organization on hiring them. The process is suboptimal. It's slow and too often insulting to candidates. Look at the questions we ask candidates – What would your last manager say about you? Why should we hire you?

DENISE: So true, isn't it? I remember being asked the traditional interview questions twenty years ago, and my kids still get asked the same questions at job interviews today.

LIZ: It is very strange how interviewing and hiring in general have remained stuck in a Mad Men-era mode. That wouldn't matter if our traditional interview process were smart or effective, but it is neither. We don't learn enough about candidates because we ask them thoughtless standard questions instead of having true back-and-forth conversations with them.

The good news is that little by little, organizations are shifting their viewpoint. More and more of them are softening their recruiting approach to reflect the reality that candidate experience is one of the loudest elements of an organization's culture.

DENISE: So, you are hopeful -- you see a change coming?

LIZ: It's underway right now! I write for millions of readers and thousands of HR pros. CEOs are coming around. Managers are shifting their communication style to emphasize trust over fear. HR people are evangelists for the shift in mindset that needs to happen and that is already happening. They teach their teams how to interview differently and also how to lead differently.

DENISE: Not a moment too soon, right?

LIZ: Not a second too soon!

FIVE QUESTIONS TO STOP ASKING JOB SEEKERS -- AND FIVE TO START ASKING

Here are five traditional job-interview questions that should get the boot and five smarter, more thoughtful questions to replace the ones we're booting.

Five Interview Questions to Stop Asking

WHAT'S YOUR GREATEST WEAKNESS?

This pointless question is defended by people who love the idea that an interviewer should be able to get inside the applicant's mind and understand their greatest failings. That's insulting. It's none of anybody's business what a person believes their weaknesses are (if they believe they have weaknesses at all).

Are you planning to share your own personal weaknesses, too? If not, why do you presume to ask the question? I don't believe that people have weaknesses, anyway. The idea of weaknesses comes down to us from our Puritan forebears.

You don't have any weaknesses -- you came down to the planet perfectly equipped to do your work here!

WHERE DO YOU SEE YOURSELF IN FIVE YEARS?

What's so special about a five-year planning horizon? In this day and age, who knows where we're going to be in five months? It's arrogant to ask a job seeker where s/he's going to be in five years, considering that you're not offering an employment contract for even five minutes. Get rid of this lame Mad-Men-era question and talk about the actual job you're trying to fill.

WITH ALL THE TALENTED CANDIDATES, WHY SHOULD WE HIRE YOU?

You work for the company. You know what the job requires. You're going to meet the other job candidates -- your candidates are not going to meet one another. Asking this question is a way of asking the job applicants to grovel and beg for the job. "You should hire me because I'm smart and hard-working!" That's insulting. Ask people their questions about the job opening, instead. Their questions will tell you a lot more about them than their answers to your unoriginal questions will.

WHAT WOULD YOUR PAST MANAGERS SAY ABOUT YOU?

Why would you care what somebody's ex-bosses would say about them? This question asks a candidate to praise themselves. You can ask smarter questions that will make it easy for you to see whether the job seeker in front of you understands what the company is trying to do and how this job fits into the bigger picture.

IF YOU WERE AN ANIMAL/A CAN OF SOUP/ ETC., WHICH ONE WOULD YOU BE?

You may have a fun and frolicsome work environment and I hope you do. Still, job interviewing is serious business. Some of the people interviewing for the job don't have an income right now. Some of them are worried about how to feed their children, and you're asking them to imagine themselves as a can of soup? It's not appropriate.

Five Interview Questions to Start Asking

WHAT ARE YOUR QUESTIONS ABOUT THE JOB?

The best question to ask a job seeker is "What are your questions about the job?" Their questions will show you their brain working, and that's what you want on a job interview. (You want them to see your brain working, too.)

WHAT DO YOU IMAGINE THE BIGGEST CHALLENGES IN THE JOB WILL BE?

You will wait to ask this question until you've thoroughly described the role and the work your new employee will perform in the job. Then you can ask, "After hearing me describe the job, what do you think will be the biggest challenges at first?" You're asking what they heard and what they think about what they heard. Variations on this question include, "What do you think you'd need to learn as a newcomer to this role?" and "What parts of the job do you think would present the biggest learning curve?"

CAN YOU TELL ME ABOUT THE WORK YOU HAVE DONE THAT SEEMS MOST RELEVANT TO THIS ROLE?

This question encourages the candidate to tell stories that will help you understand their experience and accomplishments. This question also lets you see how well the applicant can translate your business situation to their own history.

WHAT DO YOU THINK ABOUT THE WORK SCHEDULE, OVERTIME, PAY, BENEFITS, ETC.?

Every interview is a selling opportunity as well as a vetting opportunity. Ask candidates, "What do you think about what you've heard so far?" and be open to what they tell you. We waste tremendous amounts of time talking with candidates about jobs they are too polite to tell us they do not want, for good reasons that we really need to hear. The only way to get this information is to ask for it!

It is never a bad idea to stop and ask a candidate mid-interview, "Do you have any questions or concerns about anything we've talked about so far?" Don't make it hard for them to share a burning question or obstacle to accepting the job.

THE RIGHT WAY TO INTERVIEW A JOB CANDIDATE

Dear Liz,

I know you are not a fan of job interviews that use scripted questions.

What do you recommend that we ask job candidates?

Thanks Liz,
Beau

Dear Beau,

Here is a simple plan for a human, conversational job interview.

A good interview is not strictly an evaluative process. You are selling the candidate as much as you are evaluating them. Most candidates will sell and evaluate you right back -- and that's how it should be!

You will have a back-and-forth conversation with each job candidate, but you will not use a script. You won't need one. You have no questions to ask except to ask for the candidate's thoughts, observations and questions once you have described the job in some detail (see below).

1. Before the interview, you'll send each candidate a warm, friendly email message reminding them of the date and time for the interview, the job title they're interviewing for and the names and titles of the people they will meet at the interview. This email message is a simple, essential courtesy that starts your relationship off on the right note.

2. In the same confirmation email message, you will explain that in the interview, you'd like to answer the candidate's questions right up front. You'll ask them to think about the role and prepare questions for you before the interview and bring them to the meeting.

3. When you greet the candidate, you'll give them tea, coffee or water, invite them to use the restroom if they want to and show them to the interview room. You'll make a few pleasantries ("Were our directions okay?" "How's your morning going?") and then you'll sit and invite them to ask you questions.

4. You'll answer the candidate's questions. You can see that you must know a lot about the job and the company in order to be a suitable interviewer for the organization. That's okay! Every interview will teach you more and more. Sometimes you won't have an answer to a candidate's question, but you will get the answer after the interview and send it to them in an email message.

5. Some candidates will not exhaust their supply of questions before the end of the interview, and that's fine.

    The traditional interviewing protocol in which the interviewer asks questions and the candidate answers them is nonsense. It has never been effective.

    It is power-based, which means it is fear-based. You will always learn more about a person and their grasp of the topics you are discussing through their questions than their answers to your questions.

If you ever wondered why nearly every HR person, recruiter and hiring manager has felt awkward during interview conversations, this is why.

It is stilted, unnatural and pointless to pepper questions at a person when what you really want to do is to see their brain working -- and to show them your brain working, too!

6. When your candidate runs out of questions, it's your turn to talk about the job. Lay out the role starting with the big picture context and moving down to the ground level with specific duties and responsibilities, following this outline:

   - What is this company all about? What do we do?

   - Who am I (the interviewer) in this company? What is my role?

   - What does the hiring department do? How do they help the company succeed?

   - Why is this department hiring a new person now?

   - What is the purpose of this role? Why does it exist?

   - What will the person hired into this job do all day?

   - What are the working hours, pay schedule, and general operations of the department or the company that will most affect the new hire?

   - What is the training and career path like for this job and this new hire?

7. As you describe the company and the role, you will see your candidate's brain working again. You will invite the candidate to react to everything they hear, sharing their observations and/or questions. Once you get through these eight topics, you'll ask the candidate to react to what

they've heard. How would they approach the job? What would they see as their initial priorities as they walk into the role?

Why do we want to hear a candidate's questions, more than their answers to our questions?

A candidate's questions tell you much more about their understanding of the role, its overlap or similarities with other jobs they're performed and their general grasp of your company's need than their answers to your questions possibly could.

Also, in a candidate's questions you will see their level of altitude concerning the job.

Let's say you are interviewing candidates for the job of executive assistant to your VP of Sales.

Candidate A asks you these questions, in this order:

1. Does your company use Slack, or some other group messaging tool?

2. Are there some pretty decent places to get lunch around here, without a car? I'm planning to take the bus to work if I get the job.

3. What is the dress code here?

4. How much typing will there be in the job?

Candidate B asks these questions, in this order:

1. I see that your VP of Sales, Rachel McGraw, just spoke at a conference last month. That is tremendous! What role will her executive assistant play in organizing those engagements, helping to prepare for them or creating presentation materials?

2. I couldn't quite tell from your job ad whether this job is fairly hands-off, where Rachel is in her office and I'm

outside her office working independently throughout the day, or hands-on, where Rachel and I and perhaps others are working on projects together. What is your feeling on that?

3. What are your company's biggest goals for this year?

There is all the difference in the world between Candidate A and Candidate B. They are flying at two completely different levels of altitude!

Depending on the level of altitude you and Rachel are looking for in your new hire, one of these two candidates will clearly be the right person for the job.

You would never see either candidate's brain working so clearly if you had asked them the traditional, scripted questions!

Questions and Answers About the Human Interview™ Process

Q. What if the candidate has so many questions for me that I never get to describe the role and get their reactions to it?

A. That tells you a lot. If one of the candidate's questions is not "Can you please tell me more about the role" that is a problem!

Q. So, I don't need to walk through the candidate's resume?

A. As the conversation unfolds the candidate will almost certainly tell you about their most relevant experiences. If not, you can ask them about what they've done so far (at work, at school or in a volunteer capacity) and how those roles intersect with the role you and the candidate are discussing.

Q. How do I take notes or write down my feedback for a Human Interview™ conversation?

A. You can take notes during the interview and so can your candidate, but some folks prefer to make notes immediately afterward. They sit down right away and write about the interview conversation. What did you and the candidate talk about? Get it all on paper. You will reflect on the interview over the next two or three days.

Q. I work in government. We have to ask the same scripted questions of every candidate.

A. That is a shame. Over time perhaps the old, hard rules will soften.

Hurrah for conversation!

All the best,
Liz

EXPERIENCE IS MEASURED IN STORIES, NOT YEARS

We have a strange verb in the English language, the verb 'to know,' that lumps together the facts we've learned in books and the Ahas! we experienced in the stories that make up our most vivid memories.

That time I almost drowned in the lake, I learned not to swim drunk.

That was a good lesson. That time I missed my flight and almost missed my brother's wedding, I learned not to trust the car service when they're nowhere around fifteen minutes after the scheduled pickup time.

When we think about these moments of intense learning, we feel every emotion. We remember the pattern in the carpeting at the airport as we raced past gate after gate hoping to get lucky and avoid missing our flight, lungs seared and feeling like an idiot (but an idiot in panic mode).

We learn powerful lessons from our experiences – the memorable ones - but on a job search we say "I have ten years of experience in this kind of work," and people say "Oh, only ten years? We need someone with fifteen years."

They never ask the important question: "What happened during those years?" They do not ask about our stories. That is the only way to understand a person -- to hear their stories!

We must evolve and get smarter in our hiring processes.

We must remember that the most qualified Marketing VP (or Director, Manager, Analyst, Coordinator, etc.) for your company's situation may never have held a Marketing title before. This is not just true for Marketing – it is true for many functions.

We must learn a lot more about a candidate than simply which job titles they have held and which tools they've used to understand how they could help us with our thorniest problems.

We make a mistake even specifying that "The Selected Candidate" needs three years or six years of experience in a function to be considered for the job. How could we know that in advance? We could not know that.

"I am half recruiter, half HR consultant," our recruiter friend Gary told us.

"Most organizations are quite unaware of the perceptions their firms have out in the talent marketplace and among their own employees. They are shocked when I tell them that people are not dying to work for them. They have trouble putting on a candidate's glasses."

What is most important in your hiring is not a pre-determined number of years doing X or Y but an aptitude for X or Y and a passion for X or Y or some other combination of letters.

I do not know why that message has been slow to get through to recruiting leaders, but there is no doubt that it has. What you need to know about a job applicant is 1) their story and 2) what they are looking to do next.

There is no better use of job interview time than to swap stories. Stories are the way humans have always communicated significant things.

Why do you think we all know so many stories, and remember them so well?

When you can tell the story of a job opening and why a smart person with a brain and a heart would want to do the job -- selling the job and the company rather than expecting the job candidates to sell you - then you've taken another big step.

Great recruiters learn to tell their clients' or employer's stories. They hear candidates' stories and make connections between employers' stories and candidates' stories.

It is time for us to ask job candidates about their stories instead of screening them using bullet points as though recruiting were a clerical matching game. Don't we, our clients and shareholders, and the talented people around us in the talent marketplace deserve that much?

WANT TO HIRE GREAT PEOPLE? STOP ASKING THESE INTERVIEW QUESTIONS

If you want to hire great people, you can't invite people to come and interview with you and then insult them with brainless questions like these:

Stupid Interview Question: What's your greatest weakness?
The Answer You'd Give If You Told the Truth: I don't believe I have weaknesses or that you have weaknesses, either, but if I did think I had any weaknesses you are the last person I would share my weaknesses with. Who are you to me, after all? You are a person interviewing me for a job.

We are in a job interview, which is a business conversation. Let's stay in the world of business and stay out of the World of My Inner Feelings, unless you're planning to open the vault and tell me all your fears and doubts about your own life and career, too.

Lesson for Employers: Any employer whose interviewers believe that the employer is mightier than a job applicant who comes to meet them is an organization that does not believe in talent, no matter how stridently they argue to the contrary.

If you believe in talent, you treat job seekers like equals. Whoever asked a person they're just meeting for the first time, "What are your weaknesses?"

It is a rude and inappropriate question. If your company is still asking this horrendous question get rid of it now!

How to Answer: I try to focus on getting better at things I'm already good at because of course, the things I'm the best at are also things I like to do. I can make the biggest impact on my employer's business and the world in general when I get better and better at things I love to do, like graphic design.

Stupid Interview Question: Where do you see yourself in five years?

The Answer You'd Give If You Told the Truth: You seriously have the nerve to ask me where I see myself in five years, when this job comes with no job security whatsoever?

I have no idea where I'll be in five years. I'll be following my path wherever it leads. I hope you're not pinning your hopes on your own five-year-plan -- the world is moving way too fast for that kind of planning horizon to be useful anymore!

Lesson for Employers: Your job as an interviewer is to talk about the job you are trying to fill, not try to plumb the depths of a job applicant's psyche or inner life. No sensible person lives their life in five-year increments and the question, "Where do you see yourself in five years?" does not help you determine which applicant is the best candidate for your open position.

Don't ever ask this question again unless you want to brand yourself as just another boring, by-the-book, fearful business drone who cannot hold a normal human conversation and has to resort to Mad Men-era interview questions, instead.

How to Answer: In five years I expect I'll be learning something new every day and using the knowledge I've gained so far in my career and over the five-year period I'm about to commence -- perhaps here, working with you and your team.

Stupid Interview Question: We're going to meet a lot of candidates. Why should we hire you?

The Answer You'd Give If You Told The Truth: If you want me to dance and prance and tell you all my best qualities, forget it -- just hire someone else in that case. I'm a grown person and I don't praise myself, especially to strangers.

Lesson for Employers: This question springs from fear and ego. The question has been taught to HR folks and leaders as an example of a "good" interview question for decades, but it's not a good question. It's a loathsome question, just like "If you were a can of soup, what kind would you be?" and every other demeaning question from the traditional *Grovel, Knave!* school of interviewing. You can talk with each job applicant about the actual job. You don't need to make job seekers beg for the opportunity to work with you.

How to Answer: That's a great question! I might be the perfect person for this job, or I could be the worst fit ever for your needs. You have the advantage over me because you've met or will meet the other people who apply for this job. I won't meet them, but I can tell you that if I am the right person for this job and this is the right organization for me, both of us will know it! That's the kind of opportunity I am looking for -- one where the fit is very good from the start.

It is a new day.

Every step you take toward humanizing your recruiting process will pay off and grow the trust level on your team.

TEN FATAL INTERVIEWING MISTAKES THAT LEAD TO BAD HIRES

Here are 10 common hiring mistakes that cause employers to end up with the wrong people on their payrolls.

Don't blame your new employees when that happens. Don't blame the educational system or Gen Y. Hiring mistakes fall squarely on the shoulders of the people doing the hiring!

After all, you got to write the job ad.

You got to decide where to publish the job ad.

You got to screen resumes.

You got to interview candidates.

You held all the cards. If you ended up with the wrong person in the job -- someone who wasn't qualified for the position or wasn't interested in it -- how can you blame the poor person who took the job?

You can't -- you have to look in the mirror and ask, "What did I do wrong?"

Maybe you made one of these 10 common mistakes:

1. Using almost all of your interviewing time talking, rather than letting the candidate talk.

2. Hiring a person based on their stellar resume, without digging in to understand their personality, their story and their path.

3. Asking traditional job-interview questions like "Where do you see yourself in five years?" and "What's your greatest weaknesses?" Every job seeker over the age of 18 has ready answers for these fairly useless and unoriginal questions.

4. Hiring someone based only on their lofty educational credentials.

5. Failing to zoom in on the specific requirements of the job during your job interview(s). Unless you get into the meat of the job, how will you know how a job seeker views the assignment or whether they has any idea how to approach it?

6. Asking "Tell me about a time when..." interview questions instead of laying out your present situation and talking about what's actually going to be on your new hire's desk as soon as they start the job. The more specific and less generic your interview conversation can be, the better for everyone!

7. Using your interview time asking questions about what the candidate thinks of him- or herself, or what other people think about them. Outdated interview questions like "What would your former boss say about you?" have no place in a job interview.

8. Using an interview script instead of conducting a normal human conversation with the job candidate sitting in front of you.

9. Viewing your hiring process like an equation to be solved: "I'll hire the person with the most years of related experience, at least two degrees and an excellent reference from a former boss," instead of using your five senses and your

good judgment to hire the person who will be the best fit for the job.

10. Rejecting candidates who don't have every one of the qualifications listed on the job spec.

The best person for a job is not the person whose resume matches the job spec perfectly. It's not always the person with the fanciest education or the most years of experience.

The best hire is the person who gets the assignment and can talk with you about the problems you need to solve. The best person to hire is the person who understands what you're up against and can tell you stories about having solved a similar kind of problems before -- even if the industry and function were different in that case.

You need someone who is awake and aware, and someone who can think on their feet. That's what you'll use your job interview time to figure out. Don't fall into these ten traps, listen to your body and you'll be fine!

FIVE SIGNS YOUR INTERVIEW IS FAKE BECAUSE THEY'VE ALREADY HIRED SOMEONE

I met Alex, who had interviewed with the same company twice. "The first time I had an interview at that company, the HR Manager was very nice and very engaged in our conversation," said Alex.

"She told me that the job I was interviewing for was one of their highest-priority job openings," Alex said. "I had a great conversation with the hiring manager, too, but they ended up hiring someone else because they needed someone with more experience than I had back then."

Alex left that interview process with a good feeling. The HR Manager, Allison, told Alex, "We will be sure to contact you if we have another opening that is a match for your experience."

Alex was working full-time, but she kept her job search going on the side. Three months after Alex's first interview with Allison, Alex got an email message inviting her to come back and interview with Allison's company again.

"They had a new job opening come up," said Alex. "I was excited about the interview, but when I got here, Allison seemed like a different person than the woman I had met three months before."

At Alex's second interview, Allison was polite and distant. "She seemed to be going through the motions," said Alex. "She didn't ask me one question at the interview! She checked her watch several times. Our entire interview lasted 26 minutes. I couldn't understand it."

Alex didn't get to meet a hiring manager that day. By the time Alex got home, there was a terse "Thanks but no thanks" email message waiting for her. "What did I do wrong?" Alex asked us.

"I am pretty sure you didn't do anything wrong, but rather the job was already filled," I said.

Companies and institutions will interview people like Alex to pad out a candidate roster only in order to get approval to hire someone they've already chosen for the role. They don't mind wasting job seekers' time on fake interviews just to satisfy a policy.

That's dishonest and unethical, but it happens every day!

Sometimes a company policy says that internal candidates can only be considered for a job opening if several external candidates are also interviewed. That's why Alex was dragged out of her busy life to a job interview where the interviewer barely looked at her.

It is sad that employers put job seekers (not to mention their own interviewers) through insulting, waste-of-time meetings just to satisfy a pointless corporate policy, but it's common.

Vendors are used to (and sick of) being part of "three bid" programs where suppliers spend hours completing RFP documents just so that a purchasing agent can say, "I got three bids from three different vendors, and here's the one I choose!"

They already knew which vendor they wanted to buy from. The other vendors donated their time to the RFP process just for the "optics," and job seekers can easily donate their time in a fruitless exercise in making corporate weenies happy, too.

Here are five signs your job interview is fake, because the company has already decided who they want to hire:

1. Your job interview may be fake if the interviewer never looks at you during the interview, never asks a follow-up question and simply scribbles the answers you give them on their clipboard.

2. Your interview may be fake if the interviewer tells you, "We have a number of qualified internal and external candidates for this job." Why would they tell you that? We all assume when we go to a job interview that we are not the only candidate in the mix.

3. The interview may be bogus if the interviewer tells you, "If this job doesn't work out, we may have other job openings that are a fit for your background." Why would they dampen your hopes before the interviewing process is through?

4. The interview may be a sham if you've never interacted with this employer before but they rush you into the interview, for instance writing to you or calling you on Tuesday for an interview on Wednesday -- and then go silent after your interview.

5. The interview may be strictly for show if you meet your hiring manager -- the person who is presumably suffering the most from the lack of a person whose skills are needed on their team -- and then they rush through the interview, hardly focusing on the conversation.

My background is theater.

When you go to a theatrical audition, sometimes they will tell you, "The role of Jane Smith has been pre-cast." That means they already know who will play Jane Smith in their show. You can audition for other parts, but not the part of Jane.

I wish corporations would be that honest with their job applicants. They misuse job seekers' time and energy by inviting them to interview for jobs that are not really available. Sometimes it's because the role is pre-cast, but they won't tell you that. Sometimes there is no job opening at all. The organization is only interviewing candidates to get free consulting advice from them.

If you pick up that vibe on a job interview, don't be discouraged. Interviewing is always good practice, and we always learn something whether we get the job or not.

One thing you'll learn by going to job interviews is how to trust your instincts! Humans are an old species. We know in our guts when people are being straight with us and when they aren't.

Alex got a third invitation from the same employer she had interviewed with twice before, about a month after her disappointing second visit. Alex wrote to Allison, the HR Manager, to say, "Can we speak by phone before I decide whether or not to come back again?"

Allison called Alex and Alex asked her, "The last time I met with you, it seemed that we were simply carrying out a required step in your hiring protocol. My assumption is that you already had a candidate in mind for the job but were required to interview additional candidates, like me."

Allison was silent at first. "I appreciate your coming in last month to talk with us about that opportunity," she told Alex. "We were still interviewing candidates when you and I met to talk about that job, but you're right, there was a strong internal candidate."

"I could tell that I had no chance at the job, and that was discouraging," said Alex. "Your time is valuable, and my time is valuable, too."

"This situation is not like that," said Allison, coming as close as she could to making an apology without actually doing so. "This hiring manager can hire whomever she wants."

Alex smiled to herself. She had gotten her answer. Her trusty gut did not fail her.

Allison had just confirmed that indeed, Alex's previous interview was a sham. She had never had a chance at that job. "Thanks very much for your candor," said Alex. "My plate is very full so I'm going to decline your offer of a third interview, but I wish you and your team all the best."

It's important for you to grow the same muscles Alex grew. If you can tell that a job interview is fake, you won't feel bad about getting a "no thank you" note afterwards but you will know to avoid that employer in the future!

Keep this in mind: not every employer deserves you. Anybody who would invite you to a sham interview just to round out their interviewing roster is not somebody who deserves your talents!

THE MOST IMPORTANT QUALITY TO LOOK FOR WHEN YOU'RE HIRING

New employees can pick up industry concepts and jargon.

They can't pick up qualities like maturity, trustworthiness and the ability to solve problems in the moment as easily. You can teach almost anything, but if you're going to invest time and money in teaching somebody new topics, teach them company-specific and industry-specific topics! Teach them procedures. Teach them the mechanics of your organization.

Don't hire someone because they've already performed the same job you want them to perform for you. Why would you hire someone who wants to keep doing exactly what they've already been doing, but in a different room?

The most important quality to look for in a new hire is comfort in their own skin, also known as confidence. I'm not talking about fake, buzzword-laden, bravado-business brashness. That's the opposite of confidence. It's bluster -- just another screen to keep the raw and tender parts of ourselves out of the public glare. It's fake confidence. Don't fall for it.

Hire someone real, who knows who they are and what they bring. The more afraid of conflict you are, the harder it will be the first time you hire someone who is almost certainly going to challenge some of your decisions.

To overcome that fear, reframe the issue in your mind. It's not that your brilliant new hire is going to challenge your authority -- it's that they are going to make the quality of your decisions much better! They are going to take some of the heavy burden of running your department off your shoulders. They are going to fill in pieces of the puzzle that you don't have.

An old boss of mine always said "Hire into your weakness." If you're detailed and exacting, hire someone freewheeling and creative. If you're a bit of a space cadet, hire someone who will keep the trains running on time.

Hire the person who asks the most insightful questions at their job interview -- not the person who gives you textbook answers and won't step out of the standard interview script for anything.

If you want to see a candidate's brain working, ask them questions like these:

1. What can I tell you about the company, the department, this position or me that would help you understand this assignment better?

   A candidate's questions will tell you far more about them than their answers to your questions ever could.

2. How would you approach this assignment? Which issues or projects would you plan to tackle first, second and third?

3. You've seen some of the inside of this company now. We have a great opportunity in front of us and we also have our challenges and problems. What do you think we're doing right in the company so far, and where do we need to get better?

When you recruit employees in a human way, you change the quality of every interview conversation -- and improve the quality of your new hires, and your culture as well.

When you put aside the multi-bulleted job spec and hire people you trust, you stop thinking about job descriptions as boxes in an array of boxes that are supposed to fit neatly together to make a well-oiled machine. You know better. You know that human beings are not machines and that exciting human endeavors never break down into neat little boxes.

We humans can only fit together to make an awesome team when each of us has the support and the belief in themselves and one another to form trusting, human connections.

Trust is the glue that keeps your team together, and the fuel that keeps your organization moving ahead. There is no substitute for trust. We should be talking about trust and fear in our workplaces every day, but of course we don't -- because it's too scary to talk about!

When you're hiring, don't stress about whether an applicant has three years or only two years of experience with a particular tool. Don't worry about what kind of degree they earned. Focus on the person behind the résumé! Listen to their story. Your story is everything. It's how you reached the point where you stand right now.

Tell them your story, too. You are a human being yourself, not a robot. Tell them something you know you need help with.

You will never regret hiring someone who has all the characteristics you need -- and none of the "Essential Requirements" listed in the job ad. Let's be honest. Most of those requirements aren't the least bit essential.

Hire the person who knows themselves already and who won't hesitate to tell you or any other manager something they need to hear. Hire a lot of those people, and your company will win!

FIVE WAYS TO BECOME A BETTER RECRUITER

I don't know if it was ever easy to be a recruiter, but it is certainly harder now.

Department managers can be very unrealistic in their expectations. Nobody wants to say to an eager department manager, "I will find you someone fantastic, but first we have to get rid of half of these unnecessary Essential Requirements."

Managers want what they want, but you will not succeed as a recruiter until you find your voice and tell the manager when their requirements are unreasonable.

If you don't speak up when the moment calls for it, you will countless hours and brain cells looking for candidates who don't exist. That wasted effort doesn't help anyone and can trash an employer's brand, too.

Even when clients don't want our advice, they may benefit from it. What kind of a consultant would you or I or anyone be if we kept our observations to ourselves because we were afraid of the client's reaction?

If there's going to be a potentially sticky or awkward conversation about what's reasonable and not reasonable in a job ad, why delay it?

One important way to be a better recruiter is to tell department managers the truth – and candidates, too. Here are some of the things it can be hard to be completely truthful about when you talk with job candidates:

- It can be hard to talk about money.

- It can be awkward to answer a candidate's questions about the job, which can be very detailed.

- It can be tough to tell the candidate why it's taking so long to hear back from a hiring manager.

- It can be hard to tell candidates about negative or constructive interview feedback.

Everybody is overworked. It would be great if candidates and managers understood how hard you work and could take your heavy workload into account, but they won't do that unless you fill them in and educate them.

If your job involves contacting candidates who haven't reached out to you or to your firm (passive candidates), it's important to remember that when you contact them, you are intruding on a busy person's day and life.

They have a lot of other things to do besides taking your call. The rule to remember in this situation is the Happy Life Rule, which goes like this:

> *The candidate you approach is already living a happy and fulfilled life without benefit of knowing you. You may feel that you have the greatest job opportunity in the world to offer this candidate, but they are in the driver's seat, because you reached out to them.*

> *You have to sell the candidate on talking with you before anything else can happen.*

In the old days, candidates would drop everything when a recruiter called them, but not now!

The more marketable a candidate is, the less your pitch will interest them if you make the traditional "Have I got a job for you!" appeal.

They've heard it before. You have to sell the candidate on investing the time to talk with you in the first place, before you say Word One about the job opportunity.

The worst thing you can do when reaching out to a candidate you don't already know is to start interviewing them then and there in your first conversation, by asking interview-type questions about the candidate's background.

The candidate has no reason to answer your questions at that stage. You haven't earned the right to ask questions yet! Here's how you can approach candidates respectfully in an initial phone call.

RRRRRRING!
JOE: Joe Miller.
YOU: Hi Joe, this is Sandy Jones from Premier Staffing. Thanks for sending me your number. Is this still a good time to chat?
JOE: I have about ten minutes.
YOU: Okay, great! I'll be quick. We got an assignment for an IT Project Manager that I thought might be up your alley. Would you like to hear about it?
JOE: For sure. First of all, where it is located? I live in the north suburbs and I really need to work north of I-175.
YOU: Okay, this job is between I-175 and the freeway. I think it will work in your commuting range. Do you think so?
JOE: That sounds good. Not to be blunt, but what is the salary range?
YOU: It's going to be between $105K and $115K. Will that work for you?
JOE: That'll work. I just needed to get that out of the way. Otherwise I'd be wasting your time and mine.
YOU: For sure. So, what else can I tell you about the job?
JOE: What are they looking for, exactly?
YOU: They're looking for someone with a background in ERP and HR enterprise applications. I know you've done some of that kind of work -

JOE: I have, and I'd like to get back into it, frankly. What kinds of
projects are they working on?

You will get the information you need, but you can't be a bull in
a china shop about it. You have to be polite and put the candidate's
needs ahead of your own.

Setting reasonable boundaries with department managers in one
way to be a better recruiter.

Taking a soft, sales and marketing approach with candidates
(and keeping in mind that selling is mostly a matter of listening) is
a second way.

A third way to be a better recruiter is to back off on the "I am
your advocate, so do whatever I tell you" mindset that is so com-
monly (and sadly) found in the recruiting world.

Candidates will believe that you are their advocate when you
prove it through your actions, rather than when you say it.

Talk is cheap. Don't tell candidates "Trust me!" because trust
is earned over time. Here are five ways to build a candidate's trust:

1. Answer all of their questions about a job opportunity
   before you ask any questions other than "Do you still have
   time to talk?" and "What else would you like to know?"

2. Ask each candidate for their salary requirement or target
   and share the target salary range for the job. Don't ask
   candidates what they're earning now or what they earned
   in the past, even if that question is legal in your area.
   Asking intrusive questions is the best way to send the best
   candidates off to work with a different recruiter.

3. Don't tell candidates to call you or email you back if they
   haven't heard from you by a certain day. That's not their
   job. Call them back when you say you will.

4. Even when you have no news for a candidate, drop them
   a quick email or text message to say "I'm still working
   on it. Thanks for being patient and let me know your
   questions!"

5. Never browbeat or pressure a candidate by saying "You have to do things my way, or I can't move you forward in the hiring process." Threats are for bullies, and you are not a bully! The only legitimate reason not to move a candidate forward is that they are not qualified for the job or not interested.

A fourth way to be a better recruiter is to create a "tickler" or alert for every candidate you are working with and use it to stay in touch with each candidate at least once per week. Even if nothing is happening in the search, every candidate gets an update.

The fifth way to become a better recruiter is to shake off the idea that by presenting a candidate with a possible job opportunity, you are doing them a favor.

Since working with talented candidates is the only way to succeed at your job (and for third-party recruiters, the only way to make money) one could make the reasonable argument that the candidate is doing you a favor by taking the time to listen to your pitch.

The healthiest perspective is that nobody is doing anybody a favor -- the candidate is following their natural curiosity to learn about a new opportunity and you are following your natural urge to do your job, take care of your client and get paid.

Everybody is doing just what they should be doing, and no favors are being dispensed. Don't sigh with impatience when candidates express their needs and preferences. Employers write the checks but without candidates ready to step into vacant positions, no recruiter could stay in business.

Recruiting is a sales job. Selling is a process of first probing for and then responding to people's needs. You have a fantastic opportunity to do just that and grow your recruiting muscles and results, one step forward at a time!

Made in the USA
Monee, IL
27 March 2023

30623522R10089